Small Unit Leadership

D1051255

Small Unit Leadership
A Commonsense Approach

Col. Dandridge M. (Mike) Malone, USA (Ret.)

★
PRESIDIO

Copyright © 1983 by Presidio Press
31 Pamaron Way, Novato, CA 94947

Library of Congress Cataloging in Publication Data
Malone, Dandridge M. (Dandridge Mike), 1930–
    Small unit leadership.

    Includes index.
    1. Command of troops. 2. Leadership. I. Title.
UB210.M23   1983   355.3'3041   83-4268
ISBN 0-89141-173-9

Cover Design by Kathleen A. Jaeger
Composition by Helen Epperson
Printed in the United States of America

Table of Contents

1

The Purpose of Small-Unit Leadership

On the battlefield. That's where it is that you—Captain, Lieutenant, Sergeant—will do what it is our Army meant for you to do when you were offered the chance to become a small-unit leader.

The mission of the Armed Services is to *defend this nation.* Our Army's part of that mission is to *fight the land battle.* Your part of the Army's mission is to *lead soldiers and small units during that battle.* As a troop leader, that's what you're for and why you are. Your ultimate purpose is to lead. Troopers. On the battlefield.

As you study this leadership book, you will see many examples from the combat arms. But this book is not just for the combat arms. It is designed for use by *all* small-unit leaders in *all* kinds of units. "How to lead" doesn't change that much from one kind of unit to another. The missions may vary and the situations may vary, but the central responsibilities of leaders in a rifle company are not all that different from the leadership responsibilities of the leaders in, say, an MP company. If and when war comes, our whole Army will be "on the battlefield."

As you'll see in a moment, this book will describe vividly the demands of the battlefield. But *most* of this book will describe how to *prepare* for that battlefield—how to prepare yourself, your soldiers, and your unit *before the battle begins.* The reason for this emphasis is pretty simple. Performance during battle is like the tip of an iceberg. It requires a whole lot of support—under the surface, behind the scenes—before the first

1

round is fired. And the outcome of any battle is determined, with few exceptions, by how well soldiers and units and their leaders were *prepared.* Individual heroic actions can sometimes turn the tide of battle, but the real key to success on the battlefield, in any army, at any time, has always been well-trained soldiers in well-trained units. The message here should be clear. As a small-unit leader, you should only be doing one of two things:

- LEADING SOLDIERS AND SMALL UNITS DURING BATTLE
- PREPARING SOLDIERS AND SMALL UNITS TO FIGHT THE BATTLE

This book was written for company-level leaders, for those who wear the green tabs. For you, Captain, and for you, Lieutenant, and for you, Sergeant. It is a guide, a "road map," to help you build small units that can destroy and defeat small *enemy* units. The challenge is immediate. We don't know where or when that next battle will be fought. But we know, from history, that the battle will come. And it could come *anytime,* at a number of different locations. Building battle-ready units must be your number one priority, starting *now.*

Task, Conditions, and Standards for Leadership

The objective of this first chapter is to give you the "big picture" of small-unit leadership. Once you get a handle on that, the later chapters will begin to lay out specific leadership techniques and tools and "tricks of the trade." With some idea of the big picture, you can then see how all these techniques and tools "fit together" to give you what you need to lead.

There is an easy way to understand the big picture: three words. If you'll listen out across this big Army of ours, and if you'll listen at small-unit level, you'll hear leaders using three words that were seldom heard just a few years ago: TASK, CONDITIONS, and STANDARDS.

These are not just "training" words. They are also leadership words. Put together the right way, they describe very clearly *what's expected* of you as a leader.

TASK

The whole purpose of leadership is simply to *accomplish a task.* That may sound too simple, but that's what a leader is *expected* to do. He gets a TASK in the form of a mission or order, and then he gets that task *done* through the efforts of his followers.

Political leaders, community leaders, and even scout leaders are all like you, to some extent. All of you try to put people and things and time and effort together to accomplish a task. The big difference is that you are an *Army* leader. What that means is that, in the final analysis, you must be ready someday, somewhere, to lead soldiers to accomplish an ultimate task that no one else wants to do, under conditions that no one else wants to tolerate. Small-unit leaders of the combat arms will usually lead this ultimate task—but *any* of us might someday get the call, no matter what our rank or branch or MOS.

This ultimate task is what makes you as an Army leader so different from all those other leaders. It's also the essence of being a "soldier." It underlies the meaning of "service" as well, and it is the underpinning of the whole idea of military "duty." All these things mean being ready to give up freedom, and even life, for the sake of our nation and its people, in what has been called "the noblest act of mankind." At bedrock level, that's what Army leadership is all about. And that's why Army leadership is so important. An awesome responsibility.

To accomplish a task—that's your purpose. You have done or will do this a thousand times, in response to orders direct, or implied, or trained into you. Orders that come down to you through the one thing that links all our leaders together—the chain of command. The chain of command controls, coordinates, and supports. It also challenges. Think about that time when "leadership" and "soldier" and "service" and "duty" will all come together, when the chain of command will give you that ultimate task to accomplish, when it will say to you, "Attack!"

The artillery shifts, and small-arms crack, and men tremble, and the platoon tenses for the final assault up the hill. You give the signal . . . and they go. Why is it that John T. McFerren, soldier, U.S. Army, obeys your order? Leadership, or followership? Neither. It's both. Listen.

John T. McFerren assaults up into this kill-or-die situation because

a. HIS BUDDIES ARE COUNTING ON HIM TO DO HIS JOB.
b. HE THINKS HIS BUDDIES WILL CALL HIM A COWARD IF HE DOESN'T ATTACK.

c. HE HAS LEARNED THAT HIS LEADER KNOWS THE RIGHT THING TO DO.

d. HE WANTS TO PLEASE HIS LEADER.

e. HE BELIEVES HE WILL BE COURT-MARTIALED IF HE DOESN'T ATTACK.

f. HE THINKS HE WILL BE LEFT ALONE IF HE DOESN'T ATTACK.

g. HE BELIEVES THAT FOLLOWING ORDERS IS THE RIGHT THING TO DO.

h. HE BELIEVES HE WILL BE REWARDED FOR ATTACKING.

i. HE BELIEVES THAT ATTACKING IS LESS DANGEROUS THAN NOT ATTACKING.

j. HE BELIEVES HE WILL FEEL GUILTY IF HE DOESN'T ATTACK.

k. HE WANTS TO PROVE HIS MANHOOD, HIS COURAGE, HIS COMPETENCE, OR HIS WORTH AS A SOLDIER.

l. HE HATES THE ENEMY.

m. HE ENJOYS THE EXCITEMENT AND THRILL OF COMBAT.

n. FOLLOWING ORDERS HAS BECOME AUTOMATIC, A HABIT.

McFerren assaults for any, or all, or some combination of the above reasons, or for some other reasons not listed. If you had the expertise and the right psychological model, you might somehow figure out the "why" for McFerren, but next to him there's Johnson and Allen and Brown. They go too, and each for some different pattern of reasons which neither you nor they will ever know—but they go. They go because at that critical moment in time, when each will wrestle briefly with the decision of whether to attack or hide, attacking is their best choice. You, as the leader, first out, first up, and out front show them that this is so. And so they go. They follow you. You lead. And that's your TASK.

CONDITIONS

The battlefield is a tough place. Danger everywhere. A measure of fear is in every man. The noise of weapons and explosions and yells and shouts as men and teams move and fire, adjusting and adapting to a deadly and constantly changing situation. The stress on men and units and equipment is at its peak. The name of the game is "survival of the fittest." Who wins is determined by which side can best put together the skill, will, and teamwork of soldiers.

Battle is a personal experience. At your level, it's a hell of a lot more personal than it is for the leaders who are making the big decisions—like deciding which hill to take or where to cross a river. Battle follows those decisions. Battle is soldiers, one against the other—rifle to rifle, bayonet to bayonet, tank to tank. Battle is the story of how soldiers fight. And in that story are the ultimate conditions which must apply in the tasks of small-unit leadership.

What follows next is a composite battle story—highlights of a year in combat at the small-unit level in Vietnam. Two young soldiers, Stanley Goff and Bob Sanders, tell the story. Stan and Bob were draftees inducted into the Army from the San Francisco area in the late sixties. They went to Vietnam as ordinary soldiers in the ranks. Stan became a machine gunner and fire-team leader. Bob was a machine gunner in an airborne unit and for a while walked as point man. They finished their combat tour with distinction and went home.

Their accounts of combat at the small-unit level, described in their own simple and straightforward words, tell you of the conditions of battle as seen through the eyes of the man you lead.

On the day Stan joined his company, they were digging in a perimeter. They took some sniper fire in the afternoon; then came the nighttime, and Stan started learning what to do.

My first night in the boonies was pretty scary. Sergeant Ellis was my squad leader. That night he told me we were going to go out on night patrol. "I hate to take you out, Goff, but I need you. I don't have enough men. You know why? We got hit last week, man, and I lost two good guys."

I said, "Yeah." He said, "I might as well give it to you straight; you don't want me bullshitting around with you." I said, "Nope."

"I'll tell you what you do, man. You make sure that you stay alert. Don't daydream ever, man. A lot of guys get out here and start thinking to themselves 'We haven't got hit for a long time . . .' and that's when Charlie hits you. Charlie lets you walk around in a circle for weeks and weeks, and he waits until your guard is down, then he hits you." He wasn't talking about NVA; he was talking about Charlie; about packs of VC. "Hey, I really hate to carry you first night out. I know you don't know what the shit you're doing. But just watch me and stay low, and by all means stay alert. OK? I'm begging you to stay alert." I said, "OK. Don't worry man, I will."

It got dark. We got ready to go out, and I was nervous, man, I was really scared. About nine o'clock, we went out. I said, "God damn, anything can happen when I get out there." Walking behind these guys, I was flinching at every God damn movement. That was fine. The guys didn't say anything. That meant I was alert, maybe too alert, and it didn't make them nervous when every five minutes I was jerking around at some cricket or something. We kept walking. The guys started bitching. "Hey, man, that's too God damn far. That's far enough, man. Fuck it. Don't go no God damn farther . . . I ain't goin' no God damn farther." Then Ellis decided it was far enough.

Within a few days, they learned about how old-timers teach the "new guys," and how soldiers discipline *themselves.* As Bob said:

Hill was in another platoon, so I didn't have no tight partner. Everybody was your partner then. We were new, and the old-timers weren't really talking. They wouldn't give us no kind of information. I would be asking as I was going along and I'd hear: "Keep your mouth shut! You know we don't talk out here. You just shut up and you walk and you follow, and don't get close to me; you just stay ten feet behind me. I've got two months left and I don't want one of you cherries getting my shit blown away. So just keep your damn mouth shut!" The guys was really strict like that. I mean, they meant it. These cats were pissed at being out in the field all the time, and when they got the ass, they got the ass at everybody. Not just the new guys, but the CO and anybody in the rear, saying, "Why in the fuck did they send us out?" Maybe they thought that Alpha or Delta Companies got over on them by staying in the rear four days while they were there only two days. They had just a piss poor attitude in general. At night new guys would snore; so dudes would wake them up. And if they continued to snore, some dude would take a hand grenade and hold it in front of their face and say, and they meant it, man—"If you don't shut your mouth, and roll over on your side, we're all gonna die; but before that happens, I'm gonna stick this mouthful of apple down your throat. When I tell you to shut up that snoring, you shut up, man!" So these guys brought you along. But then I was starting to get pissed too, because these guys were talking to me like I was a dog, and I didn't want to be here anyway. I said, "Hey, man, just bug off." I was starting to talk back, getting into it. I couldn't get used to my pack and it was cutting the shit out of my shoulders. I was humping and swaying. And these guys were so neat, even though they looked like they got a lot more stuff than me, they were just humping along smooth as silk.

The leadership of Bob's company was doing its job—creating a spirit and pride that gave soldiers confidence:

When I joined the company we were trying to deal with a hard-core division out of the North working in the same area. They were one number different from us; we were the 173d and they were the 174th out of North Vietnam. They were not only mutilating the dead, they were taking bamboo stakes and trimming them into spikes. When they killed you, they would mutilate you, and then they would take their unit patch and stick it on your forehead to let you know that they were the ones. Their patch had a reddish-yellow moon with four or five stars right above the moon. Everyone knew the 174th because they were gung ho; everyone remembered them for the simple reason that they really kicked ass. They were a well-disciplined unit. Later on we ran into them a number of times. So the guys were worried but only to the extent that we knew what had happened to other units that ran up against them. We felt that nobody could kick our ass. We felt tough and strong, because we had a unity and harmony that I don't think was matched in Vietnam by any other unit. In fact, we not only felt that the Vietnamese couldn't beat us, we felt sure there was no other American unit that could beat us if it came down to that. Maybe we were brainwashed, but we thought we were the best in the Nam. We knew that our unit was the first American ground fighting force in the Nam. We knew that we was the only unit that *jumped* into Nam. So we was pretty damn hard-core ourselves. We knew if we ever hooked up with the 174th—which we eventually did—we could take 'em. When we finally did, we lost a few wounded, but we counted some of their dead. We were told that their documents showed they were afraid of us.

A lot of Bob's confidence, too, was because of his company commander:

Now that I look back on it, the company commander was doing his job. But he used to hump us, man, until our bones ached. We would be wanting to stop and rest, stop and cook and eat, and he'd just hump us. Some days he'd hump us from can't see in the morning till can't see in the evening, and we'd be cursing and pissing at him. But I give him thanks, too, because I think if it wasn't for him driving us on in such a way, I might be dead right today. We called him Rabbit; he was the best CO I had in the Nam, and I had two others besides him. I never knew his real name. We called him Rabbit because he wasn't like the average CO walking through the jungle; he'd be running through the fucking jungle. But he was good, really sharp. Half the time we wanted to kill the bastard, and the other half of the time we loved him because he was that good. And he was fair.

You gotta have a fair CO. You got these chicken shit COs that hadn't been through any real combat. They'd be straight out of OCS with all this John Wayne bullshit. They'd come over and want to read out of the book on how it should go, man. You know, standard operating procedure. And their book would get you killed. When Rabbit was there, we dumped the book. You couldn't go by the book in Vietnam. Maybe in previous wars you could say, "We hide behind this," or "We move over here, and this and that." But when you got a good company commander, he used his own discretion in certain situations. Lotta times the shit hit so fast, the book didn't help. It was constantly up to you to react in a certain way. If you reacted wrong, you were dead.

Take the L-shaped ambush. When you fell into that you knew right off where the major firepower was coming from. If you had a sharp company commander, he could take just one glance and tell what was happening. If you had one that got his face buried down in the fucking ground, soon as that shit started coming in, he was trying to hide from the heat, then your whole unit could get killed right there. Rabbit never got down on the ground. Half the time he was the only motherfucker up, checking things out. Where was the automatic weapons fire coming from? Where was the main body of the ambush? Then he would give you orders to move in—in the right direction! We knew that 95 percent of the people in the unit had to⁺al confidence in him; we knew that he could get us out of trouble. That confidence was very important. You had to remember that the company commander was only human. He could be out there for some bullshit purpose. As a captain, he was a career officer; he wanted to make rank. I've heard that there were company commanders in Vietnam that actually got fragged. They didn't give a damn about their men. When nightfall came and nobody could see, some grunt would take a hand grenade and just blow him away. It was that simple; hand grenades don't leave fingerprints.

We had a lot of confidence in Rabbit. He was like the Godfather. He was everything to us. His direction was our destination. Now, just cause he was the captain, people maybe felt they had to take orders from him. We didn't have to take orders from no fucking bastard. At least, I felt that way. He had a weapon; I had one too. We loved that guy and when he left us in the field, he made a little speech that was supposed to get us ready for the next company commander. He told us to drive on and stay strong, and remember the spirit of the people could move mountains. I guess in a way that affected us. We held on. Some of the guys are dead and gone and I loved 'em all. He tried to instill in us that there wasn't no black and white in Nam. You forgot about that shit. I felt that way, anyway.

In time, they learned the combat routine, and Bob learned that, at small-unit level, "war" is mostly a matter of movement, and monotony, and seldom knowing why:

Every Monday morning we'd have to take a big horse pill for malaria, which was hard to swallow. And every day we had to take a little yellow or white one. Then we'd take salt tablets all during the day because we'd be sweating like a dog. Every day we were moved by so many clicks (kilometers) through the brush on search and destroy missions. We'd be moving and cutting and moving and cutting our way through. We were moving from six o'clock in the morning till six o'clock in the evening. I don't care how many miles we walked, we never reached our destination till six. And wherever six o'clock caught us at, if it was a pretty good area, then the CO would call standdown right there, and we'd set up the perimeter. While we were setting up the perimeter, the CO would radio back to the command post and feed any information about where we were and how many kills we had that day back to TOC, back to the fire support base.

After a few weeks, we started going up the mountains. Other guys called them hills, but I called them mountains, man. Shit, I could look down and see the fucking clouds. We were just climbing and climbing and climbing. When I got to the top, wasn't nothing there. So I couldn't understand. I thought we were walking around in circles. I used to get pissed because it seemed to me we'd never be going anyplace. I questioned it, but I didn't ever say nothing to anyone directly. I would ask some of the guys that had been there a while, "Man, why the fuck we go up this hill, what we go up there for?" They'd say, "Charlie could be up there." We got up there and no Charlie, right? So down the hill into the valley we would go.

Sometimes, as soldiers usually do, Bob and his buddies found ways to relieve the monotony:

Another time we were high up in the mountains near Dalat. It was during the monsoon, so we couldn't get any resupply. Once the storm set in, the helicopters couldn't land, so we were out of food, twelve days there in the rain. Everything was wet, no chow, nothing. Some dudes were taking the C-4 out of the claymore mines and cooking just regular old weeds and grass and stuff that you pulled up out of the side of the trail. They were putting that in their canteen cups with a little salt and pepper and trying to cook it.

The CO sent out a patrol looking for food and they killed this monkey. When we got him back to camp, we skinned him. I hadn't ever eaten monkey before. Here the guys were saying, "I ain't going to eat none of that God damn monkey." "That's my last resort." "Before I eat some of that monkey, I'd rather starve." We started cooking it, and before you knew it, everybody was in on it. First we tried to roast him on a stick. We tied him up, but some people started to talk about how he was like human meat: "He won't cook good like that. You've got to cook him in a pot." We roasted him to a certain extent; we didn't have no pot. Then we cut little pieces off and started to boil him in our canteen cups. And he was pretty good, although a little rubbery, but I just chewed and swallowed it. I didn't care.

Bob speaks about the enemy—not with contempt, but with the respect that keeps good combat soldiers alive:

We never had peace of mind, never had time to relax. If it wasn't one thing, it was another. It was a nightmare. We had a saying about when we relaxed and started half-stepping: "When you half-step, it may be your last step." The enemy never fought us until he was ready to deal with us. That was what was so scary about it. He knew exactly where we were at all times. He was such a master of camouflage that he could be ten feet away from us and we'd never know it. He used all types of diversion and tricks. He would dig what we called spider holes. We'd be walking right on top of the enemy. As soon as he felt the last guy come through, or if the brush was so thick that the guy in back of you couldn't tell what was happening, within a split second he'd raise right out of the ground and just bust you in the back of the head with a single shot weapon. Then he'd be right back down in the ground, and you didn't even know where the shot came from. You'd be looking in the trees or in the bush next to you, and he'd be back down in the ground, maybe moving to a different location. He was good. "Sir Charlie," that was what we called him.

And he also speaks of the buddies with whom he fought, and how, at small-unit level, these men all blend *together* into a single cohesive thing:

We respected Charlie. And we had some self-respect, too. Half the guys didn't want to be there in the first place; the other half didn't know what the hell was going on. But since we were all there, we didn't just want to give up the ghost, man. It got to be a challenge. Not a gung ho type of thing, but it got to the point that if they wanted to try and kick our ass, we'd deal with it. We believed we could beat anybody.

The American soldier is sort of funny. He's the laziest joker in the world. He'll kick back any time he can. But when his back is against the wall, then he becomes the best in the world. Whenever we would get in a fire fight, we felt we could take care of Charlie, just put him away, if we had to. To me it was a strange feeling to even shoot anyone. But whenever we got hit, most of the people took care of business. We all tried to get some scunnions out there on Charlie's ass, to get him back off of us. And that was our main feeling.

For the first time in my life, I saw total unity and harmony. In the States, even in the rear in Nam, blacks and whites fought each other. But in the Nam, man, out in the field we were just a force of unity and harmony. We became just one person. When I first got to the Nam, I saw a lot of prejudice and shit like that. But Charlie had a tendency to make you unify in a hurry. After he started kicking your ass, your anger and your common sense told you that you needed everybody. I mean EVERYONE. That was because a few people could get the whole company killed in just a matter of seconds if they were not doing their job, if they were not sharing in trying to counter Charlie when he attacked. This was something you learned. The army couldn't make you understand. Naturally they told you, "You're a fighting team." You became a machine. You stuck together and you did everything together. You didn't have time for philosophizing. After a while, you saw it; you felt it; you became a part of it.

Sometimes it takes tragedy to bring people together. It really does. And I can't think of anything more tragic than that situation at that time. Little things happened. Guys ran out of cigarettes; they shared. We ran out of food during the monsoon in the mountains. Whoever had any salt left or a a little cocoa, maybe a package of coffee, shared it. That one little package of coffee went around to four or five guys. By the time it got to you, the coffee looked like tinted water, but it was something liquid. Being in a hell hole just automatically brought every guy together as one. It was a good feeling. That was the only thing that was good about Vietnam, as far as I'm concerned. For the first time in my life, I saw people as people. We was just us, you know, man, it was US. . . .

I felt closer to everybody in that unit at the time than I do my own blood sisters and brothers. Because it was us. We'd seen hard times. We'd seen fear. It was THE family. I mean, it was us, man. It wasn't like a regular family that may not have enough food or jobs. In our particular family, we knew that in a few minutes everybody could be dead. We was close, without being "funny." I mean like faggots. We was so close it was unreal. That was the first time in my life I saw that type of unity, and I haven't seen it since. It was beautiful. It sort of chills you, brings goose bumps just to see it, just to feel it, cause the family is guys from all over the States, from New York and California, Chicago, Mississippi, 'Bama, everywhere. At first, you got all those funky types of personalities hooking up into one military unit. Everybody had their own little hatreds, their own little prejudices, biases. But after four, five, six months that disappeared. You just saw total unity and total harmony. It was really great, man. It was beautiful.

Eventually, they became full-bore combat soldiers. Bob explains why it is that experienced soldiers often volunteer to walk as "point man":

I used to walk point every other day. I wanted to walk point because I hated to put my life in another man's hands. Every organization had a few goof-offs, some guys who weren't quite alert. It's important to remember that there was a big turnover all the time, guys coming in, guys going home, or guys getting killed or wounded, and other guys replacing them. There was no way in hell I'd let a new guy walk point for me. They didn't know what they was dealing with. And it wasn't their fault. They just didn't know what was happening. I didn't want to die for that reason, so I used to walk point. It really scared me to walk point, but I got used to it after a while. You never quite got over that fear. The point man led the company. Right in back of him was the man with the compass—to make sure that you stayed on the course that the company commander had designated. Everybody in the company depended on the point man to keep his head together and get us there.

You had to be alert on point at all times. If the point man walked into the killing zone of an ambush, within seven to ten seconds you'd all be dead or dying. If the point man suspected an ambush, he held up the company by making some signal to stop the next man back of him. When the point man stopped, the word went all the way back automatically. We tried to keep about ten-foot intervals between each man. Each man passed the word back.

Sometimes we'd know that Charlie was following us. We knew this because sometimes we had to make a couple of kills as we walked down the trail. The point man might have seen Charlie coming up the trail; so we'd hit him right then and there. Or we'd just walk up on them, as they did get careless sometimes, too. But sometimes as we'd be walking back down the trail to set up an ambush, they would ambush us.

Back in the division fire base one day, Stan came eyeball-to-eyeball with a senior officer. He tells of the importance of leadership by example:

The colonel just sort of glanced at me. I learned later that Colonel Kroesen didn't treat everyone the same. If he respected you, then you were his man. He was really a powerful man, and I had a lot of respect for him. I found out later this man was one of the most intelligent colonels. I don't mean just in military tactics, but overall; he taught mathematics, I think, at West Point before coming to Vietnam. He was just all man. Always kept himself in shape, very lean. He always had a swagger to his walk. I studied that guy from day one because he was unique. That day he didn't look at me any particular way, just like I was another man, and I liked that.

There came a time when Stan became a machine gunner. In his unit, at his level, an M–60 machine gun was known as a "pig":

One day Carl and I were walking along in a stream. Carl had the pig, and it fell into the water while he was trying to talk; the weapon went one way and he went another. I think he knew I was checking him out. I think he thought to himself, "Overboard with it." And so I said, "Hey, Carl, lemme have that God damn gun, man."
"You want it, man? Here . . ."
"Yeah, Carl, lemme try to get it cleaned up. I know it hasn't been cleaned in I don't know when. Probably won't even fire."
"Oh, man, I thought you'd never ask!" He really started painting a beautiful picture about me having the weapon. "You know, I can fire it, man, but I know you can handle it a lot better; you're stronger than I am," and shit like that, anything to have me keep the damn thing.
Anyhow, that's how I ended up with the pig. It was no problem with me. I started really liking the weapon. It made me feel powerful to have it.

A professional NCO began giving Stan some individual training, in the field, in combat:

The sergeant saw that I was really interested in it, because I used to keep it cleaned all the time. When it seemed like we weren't running up on anything, he used to set up a target practice, let me take it out and shoot it.

He taught me how to really maneuver the weapon, how to aim down the sights and keep the lead going straight, how to fire effectively. The fault of a lot of guys with the M-60 and the reason why they used to get wiped out was because they would fire the M-60 wildly. Like Young was doing that day, clips flying all over the place. He had his eyes shut, just pulling the trigger. Shit, the lead was all going up in the God damn treetops. Charlie was just sitting right down there on the ground waiting to beam our ass. So I kept the forearm weight on it to hold it level. I took aim through the big sight right on the end of the barrel. I had to ignore the vibration, watch the sight, keep it leveled downward. I used to keep it leveled at where a man's waist would be. That was how I would decipher how low I was going to shoot it. If I thought a man was up in the treetops, I'd level it right where I thought that treetop was, and I'd shoot down just about a foot below that, and I would be lethal. I'd blow the guy out of there.

The time and effort that the sergeant invested in Stan's "OJT" began to pay off—not just for Stan, but for the unit as well:

When I saw the sergeant was really taking an interest in me, I asked him all kinds of questions about the weapon. He taught me how to fire on the run, in a crouch position, laying on my back, falling down, anyway I wanted to. He just told me all kinds of tricks about firing this weapon. He was a brand new platoon sergeant; one of those smart guys. He hadn't been in the boonies long himself, maybe about a month. He was from the South, too, but a different sort of a southern guy. Didn't seem as though he was a working class southern guy, more like a career soldier. Had to be to come from the States an E-6. Figured he might have come out of one of those special NCO schools that I mentioned earlier. He knew his shit, mechanically. Maybe he was an M-60 specialist. I didn't know. The guy knew the weapon, though. I got that information from him, and after that, I developed a reputation very, very fast. The guys started getting confidence in me.

Then came the day when Stan and "The Pig," put together into a single thing by training and a leader's interest, fought in the rice-paddy country of Vietnam:

That day, as I remember, we started going real, real slow. We were riding along in a thick woody area, and all of a sudden, out of a clear blue sky, we heard a "boom bam . . . DIDIDIDIDI." The APC stopped and we jumped off and got down beside the tanks. We were looking, trying to figure what was happening. It was way in the back. When you had thirty-five mechanized vehicles, you had to figure this entourage was a huge thing—like a wagon train, it was so damn long. Of course, they knew we were coming. What happened was that one of the carriers got hit. It wasn't a bad hit, but the five guys on top of it got blasted by a shell that hit the side of the carrier. So we had to stop and wait; my squad just stayed put. We didn't know whether we were going to get hit with another rush or not. We just stayed behind the thing. We sat there and waited until the medivac came in and carried the five guys away.

Slowly we found out what happened. One guy got his arm almost torn off; another guy got hit in the eye. Damn. So we said, "Well, this is the shit. This is what we've been riding so God damn long for." We were moving toward the major conflict. By this time, we were all ready for it. "Let's get it on. Fucking bastards." We were cussing them out, all of us, because it was mostly brothers that got it that day, guys we knew. "Eugene got it man?" "Yeah, man, he got half his fucking arm torn off." "Anyway, he's going home?" "Yeah." "He got outa here. . . ." Throughout the war, no matter how you got out, even if you got a leg blown off you, you got out alive. Your time was up. But it was *the way* you got out that was the significance. That was what the American people didn't realize, how tough it was. To be hit and have his arm torn off, that was like somebody giving him two hundred thousand dollars. That was how much his life was worth. His arm. To get out of the war, his contract was his arm.

I guess the caravan stopped about an hour. Then we started moving again. We knew we had to get the assault in the backs of our minds, because the next tank to get hit could be us. So we rode along and I thought about what we were going to do if we got hit. If they came out of the bushes right now, what was I going to do? I had the pig in the ready position and I was going to sling it right down and start spraying. That was all I was thinking. The carriers were lined up at the edge of this one huge rice paddy. They started coming alongside each other but we weren't told to dismount. So we still stayed on them as they were getting into position. Nobody told us that anything was over across the paddy at all. Nobody said, "OK, there's an NVA regiment over there. Go get 'em." All we knew was that there was a woodline over there.

I never will forget how we approached it, the tanks and APCs quietly lining up in parallel formation. The rice paddy was about two times the length of a football field and about a football field in width. I heard guys mumbling, but I was just listening for a command, which could come from anyone, like the driver. Everything was moving so fast. Within a fifteen-minute interval we stopped and lined up at the rice paddy. Then the word came, "All right, dismount and stay at the back of the carriers." So the men started to climb down the sides of the vehicles. All of a sudden, the carriers started reconning by fire. They just started firing at this woodline, "boom, boom," with these big tank guns, just tearing that fucking woodline all up. Man, the whole damn woodline opened up, "BOOM didididid wham WHAM. . . ." Rockets. I heard guys getting hit from over to my left. I heard a tank get hit. I didn't know how bad.

Now my mind was jumping. By this time everybody was reconning by fire. I was firing back automatically even while this barrage was coming in.

Everyone was standing up there doing nothing but firing like hell. Pretty soon we were told, "Back up, back up, back up, we're going to be backing up, pull back." So we started pulling back. I thought to myself, "God damn. Shit. Fuck it, it's hell over there. . . ." This regiment probably had left a suicide battalion over there to knock shit out of us, so that the rest of the enemy could go on and do what they had to do. We pulled back into the opposite woodline.

While I pulled myself together, I was looking around for my men. They were really shaken up. I could see the shock in their faces—no blood at all in their faces. They said, "Hey, man, are we gonna go across to that wood- line?" I said, "Yup, I think we are." "Wow, man, that's suicide." "Could possibly be, man." I didn't know what was going on toward the other end of the column. There was our whole fucking company here, 125 men, add the cav unit, and there were 300 men, easily. Our company was beefed up and now I knew why. After we pulled back into the woodline, I made sure that my weapon was clean. That was what my squad saw me doing.

I never will forget Piper looking at me and shaking his head. It looked as if he was almost ready to cry, because he knew we might be looking at each other for the last time. And I guess there was a sort of unity between Piper and me, because politically he had tried to make every man see the full thing of what our country was doing. Here it was, just taking us to our death. We were nothing but bodies, that was all; just setting us up for this race across that paddy. I saw the hurt in his face as he looked at me. Because I had the pig, I guess he thought his brother might get blown away. I took my eyes away from him, because I said to myself, "I'm not going to think about that, I don't want to think about that. I'm not going to get blown away." But I knew that look—he looked at me as though I was a dead man. I guess he figured he would stand a chance of surviving—but the pig—everybody was going to shoot at the pig.

Soon we heard a helicopter come in. They were medivacking a guy. One of the tanks was blown away; took a direct hit. I think we lost that tank and a carrier in the fighting, so they evacuated that team. Somebody asked, "When are they going to send in the planes?" A lot of guys thought they were going to send in planes.

And then we found out that we were actually going to assault that woodline. "Assault on the woodline?" a lot of guys were saying. I wasn't saying anything. "Oh, man, these motherfuckers—" guys were bitching. Then all of a sudden we heard the CO say, "SHUT UP, and that's an order! I mean it, God damn it. Now, we're going to assault this fucking woodline and that's that." An order. Other than the original recon by fire, there was no artillery on the woodline. The CO said the next man that opened his God damn mouth would be court-martialed. We got ready to assault the woodline.

I got my weapon all cleaned and made sure that all my men were around me, and I didn't do much talking. I said, "OK, men. Primarily what I want you to do is just stick by me, OK? Emory, when I call for that ammo, I

want you to have your ass right here—you got it?" "I got it, Goff, OK."
"OK, fine, just keep your head down, man." "OK." And I thought to myself,
"This little fucker sure has a lot of balls." I mean, never once, all the time
he'd been in-country did I ever see him blink. I sort of favored him over the
rest of the guys, even Carl, because I knew what Carl would do. Emory
never would have any type of fear or apprehension. I never did even see
him swallow hard. He'd only been in-country about six, eight weeks. Here
he was, about to see the biggest battle of his whole life—and he was just
sitting there, drinking in every word I told him. He stared me right in the
eyes, as I stared him right back, and he just drank in every word I told him. I
don't know, I guess some of the other guys thought that I was gung ho,
and, to a certain degree, they were trying to stay away from me. But he
didn't. And then again, Carl and the other three guys knew that I was vulnerable with the pig, too. When I found out that Emory wasn't gun-shy like
that, wasn't so paranoid, I really took to him. He had most of my ammo.

You see, a gunner needed an ammo bearer that was not so worried
about his own head that he couldn't effectively feed the gunner the ammo.
I would be blowing lead out of that pig so quick I'd go through a belt in ten
seconds, needed a man to be able to hand me the ammo. He didn't have to
stick it in the weapon. I did that. He just simply handed it to me, and I
flopped it in there. I could do it faster than he could, anyway.

As we got ready to go back up to the woodline, the NVA stopped firing,
waiting for us to charge. It was very quiet over there. Then the tanks
moved out and started firing as they went, the NVA returning their fire. We
all started moving out too, walking at first, just walking behind the tanks,
letting them do all the firing. As the fire came in, I heard it hit on the top of
the tank that I was behind—ding, dang, ding. As the tanks started going
faster and faster, they cut us loose as they got ahead of us. Obviously, as
that cover pulled out about ten feet ahead, we started lowering ourselves
and we started firing. As they finally pulled away from us, we all hit the dirt,
out in the middle of the rice paddy, and started inching our way toward the
dike. Then we were all running toward the first dike with the tanks forty
feet ahead. We couldn't fire too much because they were still ahead of us.
So we mostly kept our heads down and moved toward that first dike, about
two feet high—high enough for protection. As infantry, our job was to take
care of the NVA who might have moved on foot to attack the tanks and the
personnel carriers from the rear.

As the tanks moved forward, they were shooting like hell, burning up
the people in the woodline. My squad was to my immediate right. We were
getting all kinds of pig firepower from that brush and all the way to the left.
I couldn't see what was happening at the other end of the company; I only
knew what was going on in the 2nd platoon.

Now, what were they going to do? The NVA were sitting back there and
waiting for us to actually try and attack them head on. What were we going
to do? The NVA's sole intent was to have us try to attack them, and they

were going to circle us and cut us off from the rear. That was the whole trip.

I was at the dike, firing like hell with Emory right with me, just handing me that lead. He said, "Hey, Goff, I'm out of lead. What do you want to do?" "Don't worry, I got enough right down here," and I was still firing. "What I want you to do is go and get all the ammo from the other guys down at the other end of the company. Find anybody that's got ammo, just get it."

So this kid, on his hands and knees, crawled along in back of the dike, collecting ammo and bringing it back up to me, and I was firing like hell. I probably went through two thousand rounds. Everybody was depending on Goff right then; Goff was the firepower. And I knew I was quieting that area, because my firepower was very effective. As I was running I was steadily blowing out lead. I saw these guys moving around in the woodline. But primarily I wasn't looking at the guys; I was only looking at the angling of my weapon and where my firepower was going. That was the only thing I was worrying about. And as I was going, I was steadily laying down my firepower so effectively that I was just not getting hit myself. That's the only explanation I can come up with.

Emory and I were running up and down this rice paddy firing. The guys would tell me, "Hey, Goff, right here, right in there, man." I would sit down between two guys and blow out where they thought they were getting heavy concentration of fire. Then Emory and I would run into another area along the dike. When Sergeant Needham hollered, "Goff, Goff, over here, man, I got thirty or forty of them, right there, right there." I'd fire right where he told me to fire. Those were the thirty or forty enemy I am accredited with in that area. Emory was not with me. I told him to stay while I ran over and was firing my ass off in this particular area, so he started firing his M–16, too.

By now we were in the middle of the paddy at the first dike, which we went over. We cut down that body of men so well, knocked out their firepower, that we could move on toward the second dike at the end of the paddy, firing steadily. After we got to the second dike, I went on firing for about fifteen more minutes, but then my pig fell apart. It just blew up in the air like it did earlier in the creek. This time the barrel did fine, but the pins came out of the side of the weapon. It just got too hot, and when it expanded, the pins and the locks and the keys that held it in place were no longer workable, and the pig just came apart. It came apart in my hands. The top of the tray popped up; it was sprung, and I couldn't keep it down. I couldn't fire without the tray being down. By that time there was hardly any activity. I was still staring at the woodline, and the guys saw how it was. "Goff, are you all right?" Emory said, "Are you all right, man?" "Yeah, I'm fine, man." Just exhausted as hell, I could hardly talk, my whole mouth was so dry. I was slumped on my knees at the second dike, just staring. The second dike was almost at the woodline. With us being at the woodline and me sitting there exhausted, and with the area completely quietened, a few of the other squads started to run into the woodline, crouched, searching, looking, weapons at the ready.

They started taking a body count. That was when the CO went into the woodline—to see if they could find any prisoners or whatever. But I'd done most of the work. The rest of the guys were sitting. I'd been doing all the running, so I was dead to the world. The guys just told me to sit there, because my pig was out of action. They got me Juju's pig; he was the other gunner. They told me to sit there while they went to take a body count, which they did. They went on S&D, search and destroy. I just sat there with my men and held down the rest of the platoon.

So after that, the main body of men were told to pull out of the dike area and move on up to the grounds of this plantation. We were still firing, taking in rounds over on our right as we moved up. It was coming out of the woods on the right flank. I never will forget this area. Did you ever see grading crews on the road? That's how the whole area looked, obviously from the tanks that went into this area. I was on my knees sweating profusely.

Then we started moving toward another dike about two or three feet high. As I went, I sort of lost my head; I mean I wasn't thinking too clearly. My helmet had fallen off and I knew it was off, but I didn't try to stop and get it even though rounds were still coming in. I didn't see anything in front of me, but I heard the tanks yards and yards ahead of us, way down on the right flank. We were told to wait at the little wall, that the tanks were going to come back for us. Three tanks came back for us. During the battle they were way in front of us. They had gone into the woods only so far and decided to come back and pick up the company. We assumed that our orders were to move after the retreating NVA. That was why they came back and picked us up. We'd blown away their line, so we were going in after them.

I was groggy, but we had to move out; so what if I was groggy! I could hardly get up on top of the God damn tank, I was so weak. Sitting up there, I saw all these bodies, or parts of bodies—hands, arms—so much so that it was making me sick to see all these bodies lying on the ground. I realized that it could have been me down there. That was what I kept thinking. I'd just look off into the woods and see rows of bodies, NVA soldiers with backpacks on, T-shirts, parts of uniforms. Obviously, the NVA had tried to strip the bodies as much as they possibly could, to try to prevent us from knowing what rank they were. They'd take anything of value. There were all kinds of dirt marks dug into the ground. From where my tank was it was hard to tell the tank gashings in the dirt from streaks where bodies had been dragged away. But you knew they had dragged away as many bodies as they could. There were blood marks in the dirt. I got tired of looking. I thought to myself, "See, that's what we were doing."

We moved on the pursuit then. We drove about twenty minutes, traveled about a click down into this deep gully. Then the orders changed. I don't know why. We turned around and came back to the plantation house on the outskirts of the original rice paddy. We dismounted and I walked about ten or fifteen feet up to the porch and collapsed. "I can't move." It was no laughing matter then. I was conked out on the ground. And I stayed there. My sense at that time was that I had just been in a helluva battle, and that I had done nothing more than anybody else did; that I had done nothing outstanding, but that I was alive; I had survived. I hadn't even gotten hit. And at the same time, I was wondering how many people were hit, how many men had we lost? I was laying down there on this ground, and I was looking up at the sky. Finally I just closed my eyes and thought, man, if somebody came along right now and shot the shit out of me, he'd just have to do it, cause aside from the fact I was breathing, I was dead anyway. I just had to lay there, just try to get myself rejuvenated. I was completely wasted. I was shaking, just out of it.

Then I heard the medic walk up. Doc took a look at me, said, "Goff, are you all right?" I said, "Yeah, yeah, I'm all right. I'm all right, Doc, just tired." "Yeah, we all are." He walked away. Then I heard the sergeant and the CO come up. I thought I heard them say something like, "This guy did a hell of a job." I thought to myself, "CO says I did a hell of a job." It made me feel good, like any compliment to somebody for working hard. At that particular time I didn't care, except that I did a good job according to the company commander. That the company commander would notice you, out of a hundred men, that would make you feel good. So after that, the medivacs were coming in and carrying guys that had been hit out of the field. I heard pros like Piper saying, "Oh, man, another fucking Khe Sanh." I knew that I had survived a major battle.

Sometime after that, back in the division fire base, Stan fell out for a special sort of formation:

One day I was in the mess hall bullshitting with Sergeant Smith and Jim, with my feet docked up on the table, doing nothing, when the colonel came spinning back through there. He looked at the sergeant, looked at Jim, and waltzed up to me and said, "Goff, congratulations. How does it feel to be a DSC recipient?" Just like that. I thought to myself, oh, wow. I said, "I can't believe it, Sir." He said, "Yes, you got it. I just came back from Saigon, and General Abrams is going to give you the award personally." My mouth just fell open. Sergeant Smith and Jim heard it, too, and they were just all smiling from ear to ear, proud of what was happening to me. After that, I couldn't thank him enough. Everyone in the kitchen just about melted into their chairs.

I had to wait another eight weeks for General Abrams to show up. I was getting apprehensive as hell. I started seeing men gathering all around, right in front of the new brigade headquarters. Finally, this captain came in and said, "OK, Goff, we're ready to go. You can come out now." As I walked with him, I felt like I was going to the gas chamber. He was saying, "Relax, man, relax. You're not going to a funeral. You're supposed to be happy today." I said, "Well, I am, you know. No problem, Sir." So we walked out on the steps, and I saw all these heads turn to look at me. By now, there were two to three hundred men out there. They brought a unit in from the field; not my company, but my unit was represented—the 196th Infantry Brigade. I didn't get a chance to talk to these guys, but I saw them out of the corner of my eye. Captain Milpas was there. I remember Sergeant Needham; I saw Hardcord Castile. They let them get up close.

Guys were still gathering. The Captain positioned me, and then I saw the brigade sergeant major, now the division sergeant major, and he inspected me. I thought to myself, "God damn, I hope it's all right." Then I saw a little smile come on his face and I thought I must have looked all right. In the end, he walked over to me and said, "Goff, you look great." He had given me his seal of approval. This was all an astounding experience to me; I was speechless.

I heard the chopper coming. That was what we were all standing out there for—waiting for General Abrams, and I thought, GENERAL ABRAMS. There he was! The chopper landed, and he got off with his entourage of generals. General Abrams was a four-star general. He had several other generals with him and a Marine lieutenant general and many other officers.

I was standing there waiting and finally, out of the corner of my eye, I saw officers stiffening up. Finally, Colonel Kroesen walked out to greet Abrams. They had a small formal exchange and Kroesen saluted them. Then he turned around and started walking toward me. Abrams was looking at me and asking questions of the colonel. As I stood there, he came fully into view. He looked at me as he walked up. As he got closer, my heart went "BOOM." I was ready for him to say. "What's wrong with this guy? He doesn't even smile or nothing." I was trying to maintain my control. I saw a slight smile come across his face. Then I sort of acknowledged that smile, but I didn't break into a big grin. I thought to myself, "Now, don't blow it by grinning." I'm thinking black, too. "Don't blow it," grinning from ear to ear, Oh yassuh, General, kind of bullshit. He had very steel, cold blue eyes, and they were very much in control. He didn't seem to be under any pressure, having to hurry up and get this out of the way. His movements were decisive. He looked at the medal, he looked at me. He held it up and pinned it on me. Then he looked at me, and said, "Congratulations, soldier." I said, "Thank you very much, Sir." "You're very welcome." Then he turned and made a quick right face. He went over and the colonel led him inside of a B-TOC.

After General Abrams disappeared into B-TOC, all the officers filed by me, and all of them shook my hand. It was all precision. It didn't seem like they had rehearsed it or anything. These guys were really pros; they didn't bullshit. I shook hands with every officer there, about eighty of them, including the generals down to the lowest lieutenant. The sergeant major of course came at the end. He said, "Goff, good job. Good job." And I knew I had done a good job for him, you know, in accepting the damn thing. It was quite an experience. It was an experience that obviously I'd never had in my life, but—it was something, it really was. After I shook all these guys' hands I was really tired.

Finally, some of my guys came up. Needham had been promoted. He and the other platoon sergeant shook my hand, "Congratulations, Goff." All officers were inside B-TOC now, and slowly all the guys were dispersing. I went back into Major Williams' headquarters and pulled off my utility belt, and then sort of eased off to my own quarters. I just sat on the bunk for a long time in shock. Every time I started thinking, did it really happen? I looked down and said, "Well, there's your proof." I just wanted to leave it there, you know. But I finally took it off. Most of the guys left me alone. They knew what I was going through, trying to come down. I was getting short, too. The medal had finally come. So really, I was over the peak.

Several weeks later, Stanley Goff boarded the "Big Bird," and went home.

Finally that day came! I was really up as it got nearer and nearer—five, four, three, two. My adrenalin was really going, super happy. The officers teased me about it. "Oh, there's our short-timer. You're not going to be around too much longer, huh, Goff?" "That's right, I'm going stateside, no doubt about it."

I got my orders to Fort Ord, California. I felt pretty good about that since it put me near San Francisco.

The day I see that Big Bird—that was all I had on my mind now. And when I saw that big plane and got on it, boy, I don't know. The feeling that you get on that plane is something that I can't really describe, like you were light as a feather. You were actually high, a feeling that you really cannot explain to anybody. You were in one piece, and you were going to fly that great big bird home.

As the plane went down that landing strip, I looked back and thought of all the guys who were still there. I said a silent prayer for them; and I said a prayer for Bob. "Lord, please have him get out of the boonies; please, please, have him get back to the States." I said that over and over again. We were airborne, and as I looked around and saw how Cam Ranh Bay was jumping into the background, slowly getting smaller and smaller and smaller—I cursed that God damn Vietnam. You know! I said, "May I never have to come back to this bastard. They ain't never getting me to come back here." Vietnam slowly drifted out of sight. (This excerpt is reprinted from *Brothers, Black Soldiers in the Nam* by Stanley Goff and Robert Sanders, with Clark Smith. Published by Presidio Press, Novato, California, 1982. Used with permission of the publisher.)

STANDARDS

Under the demands and stress of battlefield conditions such as those just described, what is it that enables soldiers and small units to fight and win? Whatever it is becomes the overall STANDARD that you, as a small-unit leader, must strive for. That overall standard can be expressed in one word—CONFIDENCE.

Confidence is what comes *as a result* of leaders like you building skill, will, and teamwork. You can't order a soldier to be confident. Confidence comes from inside the soldier and the unit. You can keep telling soldiers, "We're the best!" but just words by themselves won't work. Soldiers *know.* And they know by what they see and feel.

From a big picture standpoint, then, the STANDARD you must shoot for is something that must exist *inside* your soldiers and your unit. In plain terms, that standard is as follows:

THE SIMPLE, SURE KNOWLEDGE THAT EACH SOLDIER AND EVERY CREW IS HIGHLY TRAINED, AND THAT THEY ALL BELONG TO A SOLID, FIRM, COMPETENT, WELL-TRAINED OUTFIT THAT KNOWS WHERE IT'S GOING AND WHAT IT HAS TO DO.

What this should tell you, then, is that the *true* measure of how good you are as a small-unit leader lies not in you, or in your superior, but in the soldiers of your unit—in your followers. This is why the description of CONDITIONS showed you small-unit combat as seen by two young troopers in the ranks. When all your soldiers score high in each of the following "confidence tests," then your leadership is up to standards. High scores win on the battlefield.

- CONFIDENCE IN THEIR OWN ABILITY
- CONFIDENCE IN THE ABILITY OF OTHER SOLDIERS IN THE CREW, SQUAD, PLATOON, AND COMPANY
- CONFIDENCE IN WEAPONS AND EQUIPMENT
- CONFIDENCE IN YOUR LEADERSHIP

All four of these measures of confidence are the "business" of leadership. The last one, however, is the one that you, personally, can do most about. Soldiers' confidence in you as a leader depends on how well you can meet their expectations. Both research and experience spell out clearly and simply the things that soldiers expect of their LEADER:

- HE KNOWS HIS JOB LIKE A PRO.
- HE KNOWS A GREAT DEAL ABOUT THE JOBS OF HIS SOLDIERS.

- HE KEEPS HIS SOLDIERS INFORMED ABOUT WHAT'S HAPPENING AND WHAT'S GOING TO HAPPEN.
- HE KEEPS THE EFFORTS OF HIS SOLDIERS ORGANIZED.
- HE **KNOWS** HIS SOLDIERS AND TAKES CARE OF THEIR NEEDS.
- HE SHARES WITH HIS SOLDIERS ALL THE HARDSHIPS AND RISKS.
- HE REWARDS OUTSTANDING SOLDIERS AND TAKES ACTION AGAINST TROUBLEMAKERS.

These standards, although simply stated, are *tough.* But there is no time to put them off until "later." Our nation holds our Army responsible for being ready *now.* The next battlefield could be anywhere. Tomorrow.

That next battlefield, as our Army's planners see it, poses a far greater challenge than any battlefield of the past. The employment of new, powerful, devastating weapons of war, to include the use of nuclear, biological, and chemical weapons by both sides, will test to the maximum the ability of our units to function under, and withstand, stress. Danger, isolation, confusion, and physical exhaustion will combine to challenge the stamina, strength, dedication, and resourcefulness of our soldiers and their leaders. On that future battlefield, only the best can win.

"Best" does not equal "most." Our Army has fought and won outnumbered in countless battles. "Best" is determined by how well our leadership can put together the skill, will, and teamwork of soldiers. That's the critical factor that determines the outcome in battle. And the difference in battle—the difference between winning and defeat—is thus the difference between how our soldiers fight and how their soldiers fight. When we have been outnumbered and have won in the past, we did it because our soldiers fought *smarter* and *better* than theirs.

In any war that our Army is preparing for, soldiers who fight smarter and better are of critical importance to our nation. That's because the first battle of that come-as-you-are war, due to its intensity, could well be the only battle. That very first battle—soldier against soldier, company against company—may indeed determine the outcome of the whole war and the future of our nation.

And so, along with the standards for you and your unit, there is the bigger standard for our whole Army. Simply stated, that standard is to win the first battle. It is leadership, more than anything else, that can make this happen. It is leadership that puts together skill, will, and teamwork. It is leadership that produces confidence. It is leadership that insures that soldiers fight smarter and better. It is leadership that determines who wins. And in war, for our Army, winning is the *only* standard.

2

What Is Army Leadership?

DEFINITION

Normally, a chapter with a title like this would start off with an impressive definition of leadership that the senior man present had figured out. The definition would then be broken down into key parts and key words, with many more words about each word and each part. But if you want to know what Army leadership is, a definition is the wrong place to start. So let's save that until last. The *right* place to start is with our Army's mission. That mission is to fight the land battle in defense of this nation. And Chapter 1 told you that the only standard that applies in executing this mission is to *win.*

THE BASICS OF THE BATTLEFIELD

To *win* on the big battlefield, three basic things must happen:

1. Forces and weapons must be brought together and *concentrated* at the critical times and places.
2. The battle itself must be *directed* and controlled to achieve the maximum effect of fire and maneuver at decisive locations.
3. And, at the cutting edge of that battle, soldiers must employ their

weapons with the skill to kill and the will to win. They must *fight* smarter and better.

Army Fighting Doctrine

The three factors just listed constitute our Army's basic fighting doctrine. Simply writing this doctrine down doesn't make it happen. There is a fairly simple and clear process whereby the words of fighting doctrine are turned into the actions required on the battlefield. The process gives you the big picture of what Army leadership must do.

To begin with, each of those factors are explained in various field manuals. Some of these manuals are *unit* manuals that lay out the fighting tasks that must be accomplished by each different kind of unit. Others are *individual* manuals, called Soldier's Manuals, that lay out the tasks for each different kind of soldier. Units and individuals learn the tasks they're responsible for by *training*. Skill Qualification Tests (SQTs) evaluate how well individuals are learning their tasks. Army Training and Evaluation Programs (ARTEPs) do the same thing for units. The results of these evaluations (what *is*) are compared with the TASKS, CONDITIONS, and STANDARDS laid out in the manuals (what *should be*), then individuals and units get to work to make up the difference.

And that's the overall process—the big picture of what our Army must do to accomplish those three basic things necessary if our Army is to fight and win. It is up to our Army's leadership to make this process occur—*all* of Army leadership, from the Chief of Staff to the fire-team leader. In getting the words of fighting doctrine turned into the actions needed on the battlefield, it is obvious that leaders at different levels of our Army's leadership must do different things. Go back to those three basic things that must happen in order to fight and win: *concentrating, directing,* and *fighting*. Think about those, and at the same time, divide that top-to-bottom lash-up of Army leadership into three levels. When we match these three levels to those three basic things needed to fight and win, it looks like this:

Generals: Concentrate Forces

Generals, like those who command divisions and corps, must bring about a winning combination of forces in the area of actual combat. And the generals who are not commanding have the responsibility to make support systems work—to provide the ammunition, gasoline, replacements, and forward maintenance that soldiers need to destroy enemy forces and to take and hold terrain.

Colonels: Direct the Battle

Colonels and lieutenant colonels—the leaders of battalions, squadrons, regiments, and brigades—are responsible for directing and controlling the battle. Their job is to fit the positions and movements of forces to the terrain. They must also coordinate the mixing and focusing of firepower. As the battle develops, they adjust and adapt to what enemy units do. They make the moves in the deadly games of the battlefield.

Captains: Fight

Captains—the leaders of companies, batteries, troops—fight. Captains and their officers, both commissioned and noncommissioned, work to insure that *soldiers* fight with skill, will, and teamwork. Captains, lieutenants, sergeants, and soldiers—the small units and their leaders—are the ones who fight. That's who's at the cutting edge. That's who *delivers* upon the enemy the combat power that the upper levels have put together.

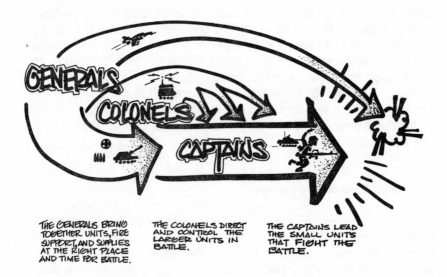

THE GENERALS BRING TOGETHER UNITS, FIRE SUPPORT, AND SUPPLIES AT THE RIGHT PLACE AND TIME FOR BATTLE.

THE COLONELS DIRECT AND CONTROL THE LARGER UNITS IN BATTLE.

THE CAPTAINS LEAD THE SMALL UNITS THAT FIGHT THE BATTLE.

ORGANIZATIONAL LEADERSHIP

The lesson for you to learn here is that "leadership" is not the same thing at all levels. Generals have no business hanging out of helicopters trying to fight small-unit actions. By the same token, small-unit leaders are not the experts in concentrating forces and in the big chess games of the battlefield. This applies in battle, in times of war. It applies just the same in getting ready for battle, in times of peace. It is a lesson too often ignored by leaders at all levels.

If you understand this idea that leadership differs at different levels, you already understand two additional and important things:

- Army leaders, no matter what their level, *always* have to keep learning new and additional leadership skills as they move up the ladder. From the fire-team leaders to the Chief of Staff.
- The better each level understands its own particular leadership requirements, the better each level can do its job, and the better *all* levels can work together. As there must be teamwork horizontally among soldiers and among small units, there must also be teamwork vertically among the levels of leadership. Teamwork must work both up and down and sideways.

The fact that there are different leadership requirements at different levels and that we need teamwork among the different levels has never been a part of U.S. Army leadership doctrine. It is now. Call the idea "organizational leadership." It does not replace individual leadership. It *adds* to the idea of individual leadership. Supports it. Multiplies it. We need both. Most important of all, the idea of organizational leadership, as you saw a moment ago, lines up our leadership doctrine with our fighting doctrine.

Organizational leadership, when we learn it and put it to work, will give Army leadership a powerful "extra" for that coming battlefield where we must fight and win, with less, the first time out. A simple illustration will explain how this "extra" is achieved.

Take a battery, a piece of wire, and a flashlight bulb. Lay them out on a table. What you have is three pieces—three individual things, that's all. Now, hook those three things all together. What you get then is one thing composed of three pieces. Each piece is different—but if each piece works as it's supposed to, and if you get them all hooked together right, you get something extra. You get a fourth thing you didn't have before. In this case, light.

This simple word picture explains the idea behind organizational leadership. In the past, our Army focused mostly on the idea of individual leadership. Personal, individual leadership. Individual leadership is absolutely essential, hard-core critical, of the utmost importance. But, by itself, the idea of individual leadership is not enough to explain what Army leadership is and what it can be. We need both. Individual *and* organizational leadership. We need the "extra."

Army leadership will work just like our example. Each individual leader in a unit, of whatever size, does something different—but if each individual leader functions as he's supposed to, and if the commander of the unit gets the individual leaders hooked together right (teamwork among levels of leadership), something extra is created that wasn't there when all we had was individual pieces. In our illustration, the extra was light. In our Army, the extra is high-performing units—the kind that have esprit and high standards and a reputation for solid performance; the kind that get things done right and get the right things done, without a lot of hassle, down in the Motor Pool; the kind of units whose drive and combat power on the battlefield is deadly and awesome. That's the extra.

Getting to that stage is not easy, but it's not magic or charisma or luck. It's do-able. The formula lies foremost in the competence of individual leaders, then in how communications flow among them, and finally in the teamwork and cohesiveness they develop among themselves and within their own smaller units and teams. Training hard, together, on the job and in the field, in all the individual and team tasks related to the unit's mission—that's what puts these three critical factors together to produce the extra. That's the formula. Plain and simple. There's no other way. There's no easy way. And the Tooth Fairy won't bring it in the night.

Thus far in this chapter, we have concentrated on the big picture so that you, as a company-level leader, could see where you fit as a part of Army leadership. It is time now to begin to tighten the focus down to small-unit leadership. This is the level that *fights*—the level that moves, shoots, and communicates. This is the level that delivers combat power, that destroys the enemy, that takes and holds terrain. This is where the soldiers are and where the cutting edge is. Your level.

THE WORKINGS OF WILL

Your main responsibility as a small-unit leader is to obtain the maximum performance from your soldiers. How well they perform depends on how well you can develop and put together their skill, will, and teamwork. You understand skill, and you understand teamwork. But the *will* part needs some more explaining.

A statement about the importance of will that has come down to us from the battle leaders of history was put this way by a wise old warrior:

THE WILL OF SOLDIERS IS THREE TIMES MORE IMPORTANT THAN THEIR WEAPONS.

And another summed it up:

FINE NEW WEAPONS ARE WORTHLESS IN THE HANDS OF TROOPS WHO HAVE NEITHER THE WILL NOR THE INTELLIGENCE TO USE THEM.

What this lesson of history means on the battlefield was made very clear by careful research done in combat units by General S. L. A. Marshall in WWII. His research showed that during a fire fight, only about *15 percent* of the soldiers in the average rifle company actually fired their weapons at the enemy. In some exceptional companies, the number of actual firers ran as high as *25 to 30 percent.*

The low percentages above may surprise you. But think back to Stan Goff and his buddies fighting in the rice paddies and along the jungle trails. The battlefield is a deadly and dangerous place. No one likes to risk getting blown away. But soldiers, for some reason, take the risk. The reason is small-unit leaders who, during training, can build the four kinds of confidence we discussed and who, on the battlefield, can keep this confidence alive. That's what accounts for the much higher rates of fire in General Marshall's "exceptional" companies.

If General Marshall's figures are correct, think of how much combat power could have been achieved if *all* the soldiers had fired their weapons at the enemy. If you figure it out, the average company could have increased its volume of aimed fire—its combat killing power—about *six times.* That means more enemy destroyed, fewer casualties, more ground taken and held. And that's how *will* works. Will is the "chemistry" of battle. Will taps a hidden potential that *wins.*

As we noted above, where the exceptional rifle companies achieved twice as much effective firepower as the average companies, it is small-unit leadership that develops will and puts it to work; in war, and in peacetime as well. On the battlefield, and down in the Motor Pool. And here, where we are talking about will, is a good place to discuss briefly the difference between leadership and management, as well as some of the things that make military leadership special and different from any kind of civilian leadership. In both cases, the factor of will is the underlying difference.

29

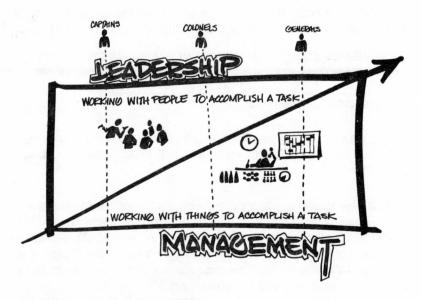

LEADERSHIP AND MANAGEMENT

In battle, when soldiers die—and in battle, some must—they cannot be *managed* to their deaths. They must be *led* there. You *manage* machines and programs and budgets. You *lead* men. *Managers* don't take those battlefield risks. *Leaders* do. *Managers* work with things and numbers. *Leaders* work with people and feelings.

"Command," at any level, will always be a mix of leadership and management, but the proportions will vary. At the GENERALS' level, more *management* than *leadership.* At the CAPTAINS' level, far more *leadership* than *management.* Look next at some of the reasons why Army leadership is different from any kind of civilian leadership.

MILITARY LEADERSHIP IS DIFFERENT

The difference between military leadership and any other kind is because of your soldiers: who they are, where they come from, what they do, and how they live—as soldiers. Our Army is not a "corporation." Preparing for and defending this nation is not an "occupation." And being a soldier is not a "job." Think about the differences:

• YOU DON'T SELECT, AND THEN HIRE, YOUR "EMPLOYEES." Soldiers are assigned to you by grade and MOS. If you don't have enough or the right skills, then you do the best you can with what you have. You can't run a want ad in the classified section. If you're short on soldiers, it means that at some time, some place, some colonel or some general or some civilian official in those levels up above you has made a mistake. Just as you do. Somewhere that teamwork among levels broke down.

- THE WORKERS IN YOUR "LABOR" FORCE HAVE SIGNED A CONTRACT. You can't fire them on the spot or lay them off during hard times. And they can't quit, go on strike, carry signs around, or stage a walkout.

- YOU MUST DEAL WITH A HIGHER TURNOVER OF PEOPLE THAN ANY BUSINESS COULD TOLERATE. A civilian leader has some turnover problems, but he also must worry about stagnation in his work force. Your worry is about the chaos of soldier turbulence.

- YOUR SOLDIERS ARE MUCH YOUNGER THAN THE MEN IN MOST BUSINESSES· Most of your men have never worked before. Many have never been away from home. All of them have to learn and adjust to an entirely new way of life when they join our Army.

- YOU HAVE MORE POWER OVER YOUR MEN THAN ANY CIVILIAN BOSS. Soldiers can be fined or put in jail for doing things that would be ignored on the job in civilian life.

- YOUR RESPONSIBILITY TO YOUR SOLDIERS DOESN'T END WHEN SOME WHISTLE BLOWS. You have certain responsibilities for what your soldiers do off duty as well as on duty. No civilian foreman gets telephone calls in the middle of the night when one of his men has been in an accident or a fight or is in jail. Additionally, you have certain responsibilities toward your soldiers' families and where and how they live.

- YOU CONTROL YOUR SOLDIERS' TIME—24 HOURS A DAY WHEN NECESSARY. For soldiers, there are no automatic eight-hour days, forty-hour weeks, and weekends off. When their leaders feel it's necessary, soldiers must work until the mission is accomplished to standards. With no extra pay for overtime.

- **YOUR SOLDIERS ARE EXPECTED TO ACCEPT THE RISK OF DEATH ON THE BATTLEFIELD IN ORDER TO ACCOMPLISH THEIR MISSION.** There is no civilian "job description" for the kind of work done by Stan Goff, or for the conditions under which he did it.

All these differences are important as you try to think about and learn about leadership. It is easy to compare yourself with the civilian foreman or supervisor or middle manager or young executive. In many respects, you two look the same. But leadership lessons and techniques developed in the business world and in the universities, though they are often valuable and instructive, *must* be given careful thought. Inside our Army, they may not "fit." And that's because of the differences—in you, in your soldiers, and in the tasks, conditions, and standards of Army leadership. There is no business firm or civilian university anywhere that has as its foremost objective the requirement to *fight and win the land battle.*

THE PRINCIPLES OF LEADERSHIP

Some of the uniqueness of Army leadership is expressed in our Army's time-honored "Principles of Leadership." Years ago, at a time and place unknown, a group of experienced Army leaders sat down, thought out, and wrote up The Principles of Leadership. They have been a central factor of Army leadership in war, and in peace. These principles sum up, better than anything else, what our Army has learned from over two hundred years of experience. Virtually all the research findings and models of scientific research support one or more of these principles. It is here that the wisdom of leadership experience and the findings of leadership research are mutually supporting.

Just like the famous "Principles of War," the Principles of Leadership are basic guidelines for *what* Army leaders should do. They do not spell out the details of *how to* lead, which we will begin to develop in the next chapter. These principles are simple, straightforward, and extremely important. They apply at all levels of Army leadership, top to bottom. Generals and sergeants. You should read them carefully, understand their meaning, then *memorize* them. A thousand times, they'll be there to bail you out when you're not sure what to do in the tough tasks of leading soldiers. You will also find that they track closely with the leadership research discussed in Chapter 1, where we spelled out the six things your soldiers expect of you as a leader. Learn these principles well:

1. **KNOW YOURSELF AND SEEK SELF-IMPROVEMENT.** Look at good leaders around you, then look at yourself—honestly. Ask yourself: What could I do better? Set aside time to watch others, to study good leading and learn how to turn your own weaknesses into strengths. If you *really* want to know about yourself, ask another leader who is the same grade and who sees you work as a leader.

2. **BE TECHNICALLY AND TACTICALLY PROFICIENT.** Learn everything you can about how to do your job *well.* Study weapons, gunnery, maintenance, and tactics until you're an expert—and your soldiers turn to you for advice and guidance.

3. **SEEK RESPONSIBILITY AND TAKE RESPONSIBILITY FOR YOUR ACTIONS.** When something needs to be done, don't wait until you're told to do it. Do it *now!* In taking responsibility, there's a special way: When performance is bad, take responsibility and hang onto it; when

performance is good, take the credit but pass it on quickly to *your soldiers.*

4. **MAKE SOUND AND TIMELY DECISIONS.** When you have to act in order to get the mission accomplished, spend all available time considering your alternatives. But, when your decision has to be made, make it! A good decision made *now* is far better than the best decision made too late.

5. **SET THE EXAMPLE.** "Follow me and do as I do" is a far more effective way to inspire good performance than "Do as I say." If you expect your soldiers to do something, be prepared to do it yourself—and do it as *well* as you expect your soldiers to do it. There is no technique of leadership more powerful than this one. It is the absolute essence of leadership, in war or peace.

6. **KNOW YOUR SOLDIERS AND LOOK OUT FOR THEIR WELFARE.** You should know far more about your soldiers than their shoe size and hat size. You *must* know what's inside them—what makes them do things, what makes them not do things, what turns them on and off, and what their needs are. Show that you care about them by meeting their needs whenever possible. Consider them as men—with problems, hopes, and feelings—just like you.

7. **KEEP YOUR SOLDIERS INFORMED.** Make sure that your soldiers understand the importance of what you expect them to do in terms of the overall mission of your unit. If you keep them informed whenever you have the time, they'll trust you and not ask "Why?" in critical situations when you clearly don't have time for explanations.

8. **DEVELOP A SENSE OF RESPONSIBILITY IN YOUR SUBORDINATES.** When your soldiers have demonstrated the skill and will necessary to do a job, then let them do it. But make sure they understand that, along with authority to do the job, they must accept the responsibility to you to get the job done right. Give responsibility in line with ability and potential. Stretch out each soldier, a little more each time.

9. **ENSURE THAT THE TASK IS UNDERSTOOD, SUPERVISED, AND ACCOMPLISHED.** Consider each soldier's skill and will to perform a task before you tell him to do it. Explain the task to him in the detail necessary to ensure his understanding. "Task, Conditions, and Standards" is a clean way to do this. Check his performance from time to time to ensure two things: that he knows you're available to ASSIST him (when necessary), and that he knows you INSIST on good performance.

10. **TRAIN YOUR SOLDIERS AS A TEAM.** Make sure that your soldiers have an opportunity to gain confidence in their own abilities and in the abilities of others on their team. Most importantly, make sure that each soldier understands how his own performance affects other soldiers

around him. If you've got a piece of the chain of command under you, think also about teamwork among the levels of leadership in the chain.

11. **EMPLOY YOUR UNIT IN ACCORDANCE WITH ITS CAPABILITIES.** Know what your soldiers are *required* to do as a unit, and know what they *can* do. Make sure that the level of performance you expect of them is not too far beyond their capabilities. Likewise, make sure that the required level of performance is challenging to your soldiers. If it's too easy, you're not stretching them out.

If you think about your own experiences, the experiences of others, and the combat conditions described in Chapter 1, you have seen all of these principles at work. Leaders who view these principles as the bedrock of their leadership will build effective units—composed of soldiers with skill and will who work together as a team to accomplish the mission.

LEADERSHIP TRAITS

Go to places around the company area where soldiers gather to relax and talk. Then listen for something. Listen for what they say about Army leaders and Army leadership. They talk about it far more than you realize. You don't hear it until you start listening for it. Much of what they say is complaints, and most of those complaints they don't really mean, but they complain about leaders because, in our Army, soldiers are "supposed" to do that. And they always have. Leaders bring the missions, the tasks, the work—and the smoke. But, if you'll listen, every now and then they'll get going on *good* leadership and *good* leaders. During these "good leadership" discussions, they'll talk about the special leaders they've known and the legendary leaders they've heard about. Now, it's not just soldiers in the Motor Pool that do this. It's also NCOs in the Mess Hall. And the company officers in the XO's office. Listen to the way these people describe *good* leaders. *Listen to the legends.*

. . . He could get 110 percent out of all of us. If he had said, "Go to Hell," we would have said, "What time do we start?" We worked our butts off for him . . . not because we had to, but because we wanted to.

. . . Our platoon leaders were good because he made 'em good. He used to take one of each kind of rifle platoon weapon, disassemble 'em, mix all the parts together, and put 'em in a footlocker. He'd do one of these footlockers for each platoon. Then he'd fall out the company, gather us all around, and time our platoon leaders on how fast they could get all the weapons put back together. Our platoon leader practiced like hell. Got so good he could do it blindfolded. He could even beat the platoon sergeant.

I was pretty good at it myself, but I couldn't come close to our platoon leader. That sucker was *good!*

. . . If you screwed something up, he'd always fuss at you, but as long as you were trying your damndest, it was O.K. But I'll tell you, if you ever got to where you didn't give a damn, he'd spot it in a minute. Then he'd be all over you like a duck on a June bug.

. . . If we had a big project comin' up, he'd brief us just like he was giving an ops order in the field. One time, he even made the IG like the "enemy." Everybody'd nod and write, and he'd go through the whole ops order, questions and all, and then turn us loose. After the platoon leader had worked out some sort of plan, he had to go back to the captain and give him what he called a "briefback." Platoon leader had to explain the company mission, then what the company plan was, and what part of the plan the platoon was responsible for, and what the platoon's plan was, and who they had to coordinate with, and who was doing what, and so on. After the platoon leaders got good at it, it took about fifteen minutes. What the captain was doing was making *certain* the platoon leaders knew what to do. It took some time, but it sure made things a lot better for us platoon sergeants.

. . . When I was a squad leader, he used to say, "As far as those troops are concerned, you're right even if you're wrong. I'll always back you up in front of them. But, by God, if you *are* wrong, you're going to answer to me, personally."

. . . In his outfit, us sergeants did sergeants' business. And officers did officers' business. At the end of a field exercise, after the critique, he'd pull out every single officer, turn the outfit over to the sergeant major, and then *we'd* take it home . . . do all the maintenance, do all the inspections, get everything ready again, and turn the troops loose. We did *all* that . . . and the officers were still out in the field, still humpin' the hills with him on what he called a "tactical walk."

. . . He sat us down one day and said, "Way back when I first went to leadership school, they told us there were three kinds of information: *need* to know, *good* to know, and *nice* to know. Now, we got a lot to do in this outfit of ours. So don't pass on all the details of something unless somebody asks for 'em. Try to stick to the *need to know* and cut down all the traffic . . . just like I taught you to do on the company command net out in the field."

. . . Anytime the goin' was tough, or we were hurtin', there he was. On those cold, winter days down in the Motor Pool, he didn't just come down and "check." He stayed with us, just as cold and miserable as we were, till we got all the work done.

. . . He didn't believe in all that wheelin' and dealin'. He was *straight*. He damn near worked the supply guys to death. But he kept 'em honest. He wouldn't let us borrow equipment for inspections. Threatened to court-martial us if we ripped anything off down in the Motor Pool. And he told the IG the truth on everything! All that put a lot of extra work on everybody, but let me tell you something. We all knew that whatever he said was *right.* If he said he was going to do something, or be somewhere at a certain time, you flat *knew* it was going to happen. You could depend on him. Pretty soon, he had all of us operating that way. With him, you *had* to be honest.

. . . We could talk to him just about anytime, but you better not be hanging around his orderly room. He wasn't in there much. And when he was, he was giving the paperwork hell. He told us one time what his "open door policy" was. He said, "I open the door and go out to where our troops are, and I talk with as many of them as I can, right there on the job or in the field, while they're doing their work. If they got problems, I find out about 'em by *being with my troops.* You guys want to see me about something, you *know* I'll be around."

. . . He kept telling the lieutenants and the NCO's to "tell it like it is." And they told him they would, but they wouldn't. Then one day at a company "leaders' call" (that's when he'd get *all* us leaders together), the battalion commander came down and talked with us a little. The colonel got through, and then the captain stood up and told the colonel just how it was. I mean he laid it on him . . . things the colonel's staff wasn't doing, and problems we were having with the colonel's SOP's. It was sort of embarrassing to us, but the colonel didn't get mad. After that, we figured if he could do it with the colonel, we could do it with him. So we did. And it worked. If any of us had a real problem and laid it out, he'd get with the first sergeant and they'd start bringing smoke until things were straight.

. . . Somehow, he seemed to know *everything* that was going on in our outfit. I mean he knew stuff about my platoon that I *knew* hadn't gone through the chain, 'cause I was the platoon leader. We asked him about it one day. He said, "Look, that's a main part of what being a real commander requires. A commander may not always know *best,* but he damn well better always know *most.* That's what I try to do. Now and then, some guy will bitch about me 'violating the chain of command.' That's horse manure. I use the chain of command to *command* with. I'll *communicate* any damn way I can —up, down, or sideways. I'll do whatever I can to make sure I know what's going on in this outfit."

Next, read. About the good leaders in times past. Learn how these leaders are described by writers who watched and studied them in detail. What you'll find is that the soldiers in the Motor Pool and the authors in the books describe the good leaders in the same terms. Same descriptors. Same characteristics. Same traits. And when you put it all together, what you get is a picture of an ideal leader. It's a valuable and useful picture because it comes from men who have studied good leaders carefully and closely, and because it also comes from *followers* who have been on the receiving end of what it is that good leaders do.

So in trying to learn what Army leadership is, spend some time studying the *traits* of good Army leaders. You may not have them all yourself. And even if you did, that wouldn't guarantee you would be a good leader. But what these traits do is give you a summary picture of what people—mostly followers of all ranks—think a good leader should be. Writers wrote about them, but they came mostly from followers—Army followers of all ranks, talking about the best leaders they had ever known. In war, and in peace. On the battlefield, and down in the Motor Pool.

Now, if you memorized those Principles of Leadership, think back to the very first principle. The leadership traits, which are listed and explained below, will give you the best possible tool for putting that first principle to work.

There are sixteen leadership traits that you should focus on when you put that first principle to work. Remember, however, that the way you see yourself may not be the way your soldiers actually see you. As you read through the self-evaluation checklist for each of the traits, be honest with yourself—try to stand back and see yourself as your soldiers see you.

1. **COURAGE,** demonstrated by

   - Taking risks—on the battlefield in war, and with your boss in peace.
   - Acting calmly and firmly in stressful situations.
   - Standing up for what is right, regardless of what others may think.
   - Accepting personal responsibility for your mistakes, and for your orders—not blaming unpleasant orders on "they."
   - Making full-bore efforts toward mission accomplishment, even in the face of major obstacles and problems.
   - Making on-the-spot corrections of soldiers who need correcting. Anywhere.

2. **BEARING,** demonstrated by

   - Setting and maintaining high standards of appearance.
   - Avoiding use of excessive profanity.
   - Controlling your voice and gestures so that extremes of emotion don't show in your actions, except at the times you carefully choose.

3. **DECISIVENESS,** demonstrated by

   - Studying your alternatives and carefully selecting the best course of action—when time permits.

- Picking alternatives and making decisions quickly when there is no time for careful study.
- Knowing when *not* to make a decision.

4. **DEPENDABILITY,** demonstrated by

- Being places on time when you're told to be there or when you say you will.
- Doing those tasks that you've been told to do and those tasks that you've promised to do—in a complete and timely manner.

5. **ENDURANCE,** demonstrated by

- Maintaining the physical and mental stamina to perform your duties under stress conditions and for extended periods of time.

6. **ENTHUSIASM,** demonstrated by

- Consistently communicating a positive attitude to your soldiers.
- Never complaining *in front of your soldiers* about "they" or "the system."
- Emphasizing to your soldiers their *successes.*
- Explaining to your soldiers why they must perform the tasks expected of them—in terms they can understand and accept.
- Encouraging your soldiers to take the initiative to overcome obstacles to performance.

7. **HUMILITY,** demonstrated by

- Ensuring your soldiers receive the credit due them when they perform well.
- Emphasizing to your soldiers how important *they* are to the unit.
- Describing your unit's performance in terms of "what *we* did," instead of "what *I* did."

8. **HUMOR,** demonstrated by

- Having fun doing your job.
- Joking when the going gets tough.

9. **INITIATIVE,** demonstrated by

- Taking action in situations where something must be done, even in the absence of direction from a superior.
- Looking for and figuring out better ways to do things.
- Planning ahead.

10. **INTEGRITY,** demonstrated by

- Telling the truth, to both your superiors and your soldiers.
- Using your power to work for mission accomplishment or for your soldiers—not for your own personal or private gain.

- Encouraging honest and open communication in your unit.

11. **JUDGMENT,** demonstrated by

   - Closely considering a *range* of alternatives before you act.
   - Thinking out the possible effects of what you're about to do *before* you do it.

12. **JUSTICE,** demonstrated by

   - Consistent application of rewards and punishment to all soldiers in your unit.
   - Making decisions that support mission accomplishment and that *also* take into account the needs of your soldiers.
   - Listening to all sides of an issue before making a decision that affects your soldiers.

13. **KNOWLEDGE,** demonstrated by

   - Making sound tactical decisions.
   - Performing administrative and technical duties *well*.
   - Recognizing and correcting inadequate performance of your soldiers.
   - Showing your soldiers *yourself* how *they* should perform their duties.

14. **TACT,** demonstrated by

   - Speaking to others (superiors and subordinates) with the same kind of respect that you expect yourself.

15. **LOYALTY,** demonstrated by

   - Passing on and carrying out the tough orders of superiors without expressing personal criticism.
   - Defending your soldiers against unfair treatment from outside or above.
   - Discussing problems in your unit and the problems of your soldiers only with those individuals who can help solve the problems.

16. **SELFLESSNESS,** demonstrated by

   - Ensuring that the needs of your soldiers are met before attending to your own needs.
   - Sharing hardship, danger, and discomfort with your soldiers.
   - Taking every action possible to provide for the welfare of your soldiers.

The responsibility for developing your leadership abilities rests squarely on your shoulders. Good leaders are "made"—not born. But the making of a good leader involves dedication, hard work, and a willingness to try out new skills and techniques as you grow and develop. Becoming a good leader also requires that you accept the fact that soldiers don't follow just stripes and bars—soldiers follow *leaders* who wear stripes and bars.

When the chips are down, your soldiers will look at you as a person. They'll look right through your insignia—to your skill, and to your will, and to your heart and your mind. They'll judge you based on a set of standards that looks pretty much like these traits we've discussed. All that in a fraction of a second. And then—if you measure up pretty well—they'll take the risk.

DEFINITION OF ARMY LEADERSHIP

As we end this chapter, you should have a pretty good idea of what just words, by themselves, can tell you about, "What is Army leadership?" You have the big picture. You know that the primary objective of Army leadership (of which you are a part) is to fight and win the land battle. You know that our battle doctrine and our leadership doctrine are linked together and are mutually supporting. You have some understanding of the idea of "organizational" leadership. You know that leadership and management are not the same. You know that our Army, and its soldiers, are something different, something special. You have a set of principles which, if you'll just flat-out memorize them, will always be there to give you good guidance when you get confused or when the going gets tough. And finally, you have a list of traits or descriptors, a set of standards, based on the expectations and needs of those who must follow you when you lead. All of this big picture is *part* of what Army leadership is.

From here on out in the chapters that follow, we move to the specifics of how to lead at small-unit level. Like our basic leadership doctrine and our basic principles of leadership, the content of these specifics is a combination of two things: the wisdom of leadership experience and the findings of scientific research—boiled down to the basics and put in plain words. *Learn* in detail what's in here. Then *use* the checklists, guidelines, and techniques—they've all been tried out, and they all work. When you've done that, then you'll *know* what Army leadership is and how it works at company, battery, and troop level. And that's better than any words that any person can write in any definition.

How to Figure Out the Right Things to Do

THE "GOLDEN RULE" FOR DOING THE *RIGHT* THINGS

In trying to sort out "what to do as a leader," whether you're tackling a specific requirement from your own leader or thinking about the overall task of small-unit leadership, there is a basic piece of leadership philosophy to guide you. This philosophy says, first, that you should try to do things *right*—in accordance with the standards established. But there's more. Almost anyone, with enough supervision, can follow a written-out step-by-step procedure. Your soldiers do it every day with the tasks, conditions, and standards of their Soldier's Manuals. Your challenge as a leader is to do things right but, more importantly, to also do the *right* things.

How do you decide which are the right things to do? Tough. But there is a "Golden Rule"—a start point to which you can always go back. A thousand times, when you have some leeway to decide what to do, "the start point of company-level leadership" will help you begin to sort out the *right* things from among all the possible alternatives, competing demands, and shifting priorities. The start point is simple. We've mentioned it several times before. It goes like this:

The primary objective of our Army is *to win the land battle.* In support of this objective, captains, lieutenants, and sergeants have two basic responsibilities:

- LEADING SOLDIERS AND SMALL UNITS DURING BATTLE
- PREPARING SOLDIERS AND SMALL UNITS TO FIGHT
  THE BATTLE

THE COMPANY

With these ideas as the start point for deciding what to do, let's next take a look at the company. It is often called a "unit." If you'll look that word up, you'll find that a unit is a "one," a whole composed of *parts put together,* a single thing.

Now picture this "thing" on the battlefield. It came there to *fight.* Its sole purpose in life is to destroy enemy and to take and hold ground. It was designed that way. It was designed, like you, by evolution. It is the result of countless centuries of adjusting and adapting to the demands of thousands of battles. In each of those battles, the fittest survived. And that "thing" there on the battlefield is the result of all those lessons learned back across all those centuries. It is there on the battlefield for one reason—to fight. Its standard is simple: SURVIVE. And on the battlefield, that means only one thing: **WIN.**

This "thing" can move across country at 3–10 miles an hour. When it moves, it stretches out like a snake in a line about a mile long. When it rests, it curls up, facing outward, ready to fight, in a circle about three hundred yards across. If it rests for very long, it begins to disappear down into the earth. On the battlefield, when it's fighting, it eats 2,028 cans of C rations in a day. Drinks about 507 gallons of water. And it never sleeps.

When this thing attacks, its destructive power is awesome. It can come from any direction, day or night. It can hit head-on, but usually it won't do that. It will instead send out pieces of itself in the night to sense out the weak and unprotected places ahead of time, then at dawn, it will strike. It kills mostly by firing steel projectiles into the vital organs and critical parts of its opponents. In a day of sustained combat, it can deliver thirty thousand of these projectiles, of all shapes and sizes. Many of these projectiles explode and shatter on contact, each creating a thousand more fragments of steel that search for those vital organs.

Very seldom does this thing fight by itself. In battle, it calls its kin, and they come—other "things" that look just like it, others that move at high speeds in steel machines, some that fly and some that just stand back and shoot, all of them *delivering steel* into vital organs.

This thing, like you, is alive. Like you, it has muscles—called soldiers. Like you, it has a brain—called the Company CP. And like you, it has, linked to that brain, a nervous system that carries the information that controls and coordinates the muscles, and this is called *the leadership* of the unit—the captain, the lieutenants, the sergeants. How well this thing fights, how well it can deliver steel, depends upon the muscles *and* the nerves. And upon whether *both* function as they are supposed to. And, finally and mostly, upon how well and how much they have practiced *together.*

In the least complex and most humble of all the kinds of fighting companies in our Army today, there are 169 men. For each of these men, there are 66 items of clothing and equipment that belong to him. There are 20 more items of clothing and equipment that the company gives to each man. And the company itself has 866 more major items of equipment and weapons that the 169 men use when the whole unit fights. Most of these items that belong to the company are for the purpose of delivering steel.

If the unit is to do what it's supposed to do on the battlefield—fight and win—it needs to know how to use all of these weapons and items of equipment efficiently and effectively. How well it does this depends greatly on how much SKILL the unit has. If the unit is fully trained and ready to fight, it knows fifteen hundred different kinds of individual skills. And it can combine these individual skills into about six hundred more packages of skill that are used by the company's squads and platoons and by the company itself. That's more than two thousand different skills. Soldiers and teams use all these skills to put the weapons and equipment to work to win. And there are other "things" like artillery batteries, tank companies, cavalry troops, and air defense units. All have special capabilities—and they can join with each other to become a larger thing called "The Combined Arms Team" with at least ten thousand different skills.

All these numbers tell you how complicated that "thing" is on the inside and why it is so deadly. The leadership of the unit, which we have called the nervous system, is what organizes and coordinates the whole complex, deadly lash-up.

THREE BASIC LEADERSHIP PROCEDURES

On the battlefield, this nervous system works in a specific way. There is a step-by-step procedure that our Army learned about three or four wars ago. It works. It wins. It is a *basic* in the business of knowing what to do

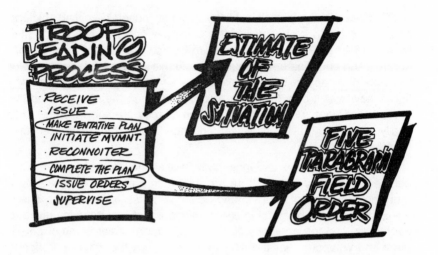

and getting it done. There are scientific names for this procedure, but our Army calls it **THE TROOP-LEADING PROCESS.**

- RECEIVE THE MISSION. (Get the orders for what the unit is going to do.)
- ISSUE THE WARNING ORDER. (Alert subordinates so they can start getting ready.)
- MAKE A TENTATIVE PLAN. (Figure out a general, "ballpark" plan.)
- INITIATE NECESSARY MOVEMENT. (Start troops moving toward where the action will be.)
- RECONNOITER. (Make an on-the-ground study of where the action will take place.)
- COMPLETE THE PLAN. (Adjust the "ballpark" plan and fill in the details.)
- ISSUE ORDERS. (Communicate the plan to subordinates and check for understanding.)
- SUPERVISE AND REFINE. (Keep checking on how the action is going, and keep making adjustments.)

If you're a good small-unit leader, you've got this with you right now on a small card in your wallet or notebook. If you're among the *best* small-unit leaders, you don't need this written down. It is more than something you have merely learned. It is, if you're among the best, an instinct. Automatic.

Some leaders think this troop-leading process is a guide for "what to do" in a field exercise, or when the unit fights. No. This process will work *all* the time—on the battlefield taking an objective or down in the Motor

Pool getting ready for a big inspection. In peacetime, you might have to change a few words here and there. But this is the basic process by which the leadership of the unit gets the *right* things done. Big things, and little things.

Let's go back now and look very carefully at some of the steps in that basic process. There are, in several of those steps, some more specific *how-to's* for determining "what to do."

Two of the steps of THE TROOP-LEADING PROCESS flat-out require you to know how to plan. How do you do that in the best, easiest, and quickest way? You use another basic step-by-step process that becomes, among the best leaders, an instinct. It, too, has been around a long time because it works, and wins. It is a *how-to* for the planning required in THE TROOP-LEADING PROCESS. Our Army calls it **THE ESTIMATE OF THE SITUATION.**

- MISSION (What we must accomplish)
- SITUATION (What's going on around us)
- COURSES OF ACTION (Ways to accomplish the Mission)
- AN ANALYSIS OF COURSES OF ACTION (How the "ways" look)
- COMPARISON OF COURSES OF ACTION (Which ways are better)
- DECISION AND CONCEPT OF OPERATION (How to execute the chosen way)

And this basic, too, will work in war and in peace. On the battlefield, it will tell you how to *plan* for the patrols that will sense out the weak and unprotected places in an enemy unit. In peacetime, it will tell you how to *plan* for the best way to train your 81mm mortars to shoot HE missions at night and, simultaneously, fire their own illumination rounds. The ESTI-MATE walks you through the best possible planning process—the one which is most likely to lead to your choosing the *right* things to do. When the ESTIMATE is an instinct, the whole thing and all the parts may take only a few seconds.

Next, go back and look at Step 7 of THE TROOP-LEADING PRO-CESS—where it says ISSUE ORDERS. There are two things to know about this particular step. First, this is the precise point where the nerves of the nervous system are hooked to each other. This is the track of the chain of command. This is where the leadership of the unit is linked to-gether. When the captain reaches his seventh step in THE TROOP-LEADING PROCESS, the lieutenants then have the information they need to begin *their* first step. And when the lieutenants complete their planning and reach the seventh step, the sergeants can begin the pro-cess that *leads* the soldiers—moves the muscles.

All this might appear to be a time-consuming process. First time out, it is. But when all the levels of the leadership in the unit use this same process, and when they have run a hundred missions together, the "vertical teamwork" that we mentioned in Chapter 2 begins to develop. Procedures that had to be thought through and worked out before now become SOP. Automatic. And what is written down in the notebooks and on the wallet cards of the leadership begins to become instinct.

The second thing about ISSUE ORDERS is how to do it. Go back in THE TROOP-LEADING PROCESS to where you were trying to get started with your planning. How good your planning is depends heavily on how good the information was when the next higher level issued orders to you. Too little information, and *your* planning is incomplete. Too much information, and you have trouble separating the "need to know" from the "nice to know." When you do get it separated out, you've used precious time needed by the leaders and the soldiers below you. And finally, if you got the wrong information, your planning may well lead to doing the wrong things.

By studying the battles of history and the results of scientific research, leaders have learned that this passing of orders from one level to the next is the most critical of all the processes performed by the leadership of the unit. For this reason, there is a specific format for issuing orders down through the levels. It dovetails with THE TROOP-LEADING PROCESS and THE ESTIMATE OF THE SITUATION. This format is designed to provide the *essential and accurate information* that a subordinate leader needs to start *his* troop-leading process. Our Army calls it **THE FIVE-PARAGRAPH FIELD ORDER.** Like the other two, it is a basic in the process of determining what to do and getting it done.

- SITUATION (What's going on)
- MISSION (What we have to do)
- EXECUTION (How we're going to do it)
- SERVICE SUPPORT (Supply, maintenance, ammo, etc.)
- COMMAND AND SIGNAL (CP and Commo arrangements)

You have heard of all three of these basic procedures before, at wherever it was you were first trained to be a leader. If you chalked them up as some special "what to do's" for use in field exercises, you missed the boat. Each of these three time-proven and battle-tested basics is designed carefully to ensure the smoothest possible functioning of the nervous system when that "thing" does its thing on the battlefield. Each of these three basic procedures is designed specifically to support the other two. All have the same all-important word in common: **MISSION.**

And, because these three procedures were designed to get the right thing done under the toughest conditions imaginable, they can handle *any* peacetime mission or task.

Today, adapt these basics a little to fit the missions and tasks you have *right now,* then use them and continue to use them until they become instinct. You'll do a far better job as a leader in figuring out what to do—and getting it *done.* Guaranteed—by the wisdom of leadership experience and the facts of leadership research—to get more of the right things done and to cut down on the chances of wasting the effort, energy, time, and lives of subordinates and soldiers.

THE CHAIN OF COMMAND

You are going to learn some things about the chain of command right now that you never knew before. You already know that it lays out very clearly the line of legal authority from the President of the United States right down to you. It spells out who has authority to issue orders to whom. It identifies for anyone, at any level, who is "in charge." More important, it also identifies who is *responsible* for getting tasks done and for taking care of those who do them. A chain of command is an absolute essential for getting done, in an organized way, any task that requires the effort of more than one person. That is a flat-out fact. What this should tell you, as a *leader,* is that here—in this discussion of the chain of command and how it works—is another basic.

For now, never mind the links of the chain that run up through those upper levels of leadership and on up to the President. Think about the links in the company. We have called this *the leadership* of the unit: the captain, lieutenants, sergeants. The leadership is the nervous system, or the channel of communication that coordinates and controls, the thing that puts together skill, will, and teamwork, all that equipment and all those weapons, the thing that focuses combat power. Why is the chain of command so important? Well, as is true for almost everything else in our Army, if you want to know the reason and purpose of something, go to the battlefield, where that "thing" fights. The "why" for *anything* must always be answered there.

In the company, on the battlefield, there is no time for silly arguments and discussion about who takes orders from whom, which orders to follow, what the objectives ought to be, or what standards should be established. Any of this wastes time and destroys the quick, smooth coordination that the unit must have if it is to *win* in the deadly business of delivering steel. On the battlefield, the formal chain has been established by law and TO&E; leaders have been appointed by the commander to hold designated leadership positions; and authority, responsibility, and obedience are *facts.* All that's settled. What the chain of command does on the battlefield is COMMUNICATE.

We will, in Chapter 7, spend considerable time on the techniques of how to communicate. But communication on the battlefield is not quite the same thing. In battle, the chain of command is the main channel, the prime line, of the communications, the information, that must flow among all the parts of the company so it can fight as a *unit,* as a whole "thing."

The chain of command coordinates and controls. And to do this, it must move *information* up and down among the levels of the leadership of the unit. The chain of command moves battle information—quickly, clearly, cleanly, completely, and only the critical, and only the truth. It is the nervous system of the unit. And when it has breakdowns or failures, the unit, just like you, will go to pieces and lose—and die. This simple fact of the battlefield explains many things.

It tells you why there are *prescribed* hand and arm signals. It tells you why there is a *prescribed* language for the radios and telephones and why experienced leaders will discipline this carefully. It tells you why you should learn, use, and make instinctive and habitual those three basic procedures we discussed a moment ago. They are the main words in the "language" of a chain of command communicating in battle. And finally, it tells you why our older, wiser, experienced leaders are always so concerned about "working through the chain." What these leaders *know* is that the development, functioning, and maintenance of the chain of command in peacetime is the major determinant of whether or not the unit will survive and win in battle.

As a leader, you are a link in the chain of command. This, as you know, means far more than having a green tab or a position on the organizational chart. When that unit fights, you do many things, but the most important thing you do is communicate—*get, process,* and *move* information both up and down. In a smoothly functioning chain of command working hard at delivering steel, there are only two kinds of information moving downward in the chain, and two kinds moving up.

Flowing downward are *orders*—information that controls. You might get a whole written-out FIVE-PARAGRAPH FIELD ORDER, brought by a runner. Or you might get a frag order coming over the radio from your leader as he makes the inevitable changes and adjustments called for in that final step of good troop-leading procedure. The other kind of information moving downward is *planning information*—the kind that you as a subordinate need for your own planning, for coordinating with other parts of the unit, and for figuring out ahead of time "what to do" next.

Moving upward in the chain, there are, first and most important, *reports* such as enemy sightings, status reports, SITREPS, and locations. Reports tell the "brain" what's happening inside the unit—what all the parts are seeing and doing and what kind of shape they're in. More important, these reports moving upward describe the progress in carrying out the orders that came down before. The second kind of information moving upward is *requests* for support—which parts of the unit need more of what to carry out their orders. This is what happened back there when the "thing" called its kin.

And that's what takes place when the chain communicates and the unit fights—mainly two kinds of information moving down and two kinds of information moving up. This information doesn't flow along through a pipe. It comes in many forms: Messages on paper. Runners. Hand and arm signals. Smoke grenades and flares. Radios and telephones. And most often at your level, by men yelling and shouting and calling to each other. This is how the chain of command communicates, tells a *unit* "what to do." Way back in Chapter 1, the bottom link in the chain communicated a single thought to McFerren: "Attack!" And he did it.

<u>YOU</u> AS A LINK IN THE CHAIN OF COMMAND

You, as a leader, are *vital, critical,* when that battle information starts flowing up and down the chain of command. Again, the most important thing you do as a link in the chain is COMMUNICATE—*get, process,* and *move* information. Now at this point, we can develop some how-to's about these three tasks.

First off and flat out, you as a leader must be "expert" in the nomenclature, functioning, operation, and maintenance of *any* piece of communications equipment and *any* communications procedure used or likely to be used at your level. For you as a leader, this is far more important than being "expert" with your individual weapon. There is no qualification badge for being "expert" in communication. That's one of the things that the term "NCO" or "officer" stands for automatically.

Getting information does not mean waiting until it's given to you. If it's needed, you get it. From above or below. This says that you, as a link in the chain of command, need to be thinking constantly about what information is *needed* by the link above you and the link below you. Getting does not mean just receiving. What you get, from above or below, may have errors in it. Or you may not understand it. In either case, *think,* and compare what you get with what you already know and remember. If it

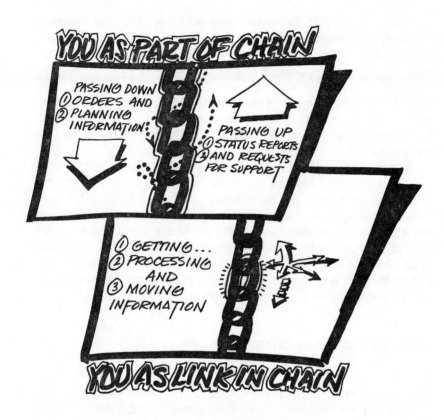

doesn't seem right, or you don't understand it clearly, go back to where you got it and check. If you've lost communications completely and can't get any information, then first think of what it is your leader is trying to accomplish, then do what YOU think is the right thing to do.

A "remote" radio set sitting up on a hill somewhere can pass on, unchanged, all the information it gets, going up or going down. But remote sets aren't links in the chain of command. You, as a leader, *process* the information—use it, do things with it. If you *get* a FIVE-PARA-GRAPH FIELD ORDER, you *process* the information by running it through the ESTIMATE. Then you move that information on when *you* issue orders.

Most of the time, good *processing* requires that you cut out some of the information you get before you pass it up or down. This is tricky. Remote units can't do it. To cut out what should be cut out, you have to know the information needs of the link above and the link below. Then you can answer this question: Which information is **need-to-know,** which is **good-to-know,** and which is **nice-to-know?** If time is critical and things are moving fast, then cut out the "nice" and the "good."

Processing also means that you must often change information—not the meaning or the truth of the information, but often the words or the language or the way the information is carried—so that the next link up above or down below can *understand* it. You "translate." A frag order comes down to you as a bunch of words on the radio, and you translate that into a hand-and-arm signal for the next link below. The *meaning* of the words and the signal was the same: "Attack!"

Moving information means you don't sit on it. If you made a conscious decision to *stop* some item of information while you were cutting down and translating, that's fine. But, if you know the information needs of the links above and below, then you know what's critical. And if what you have is hot, then it's got to move with speed and accuracy—like a reflex action in the nervous system of a well-trained athlete.

Speed is determined mainly by how important you think "communications" is and by how "expert" you are with communications equipment, procedures, and techniques. And accuracy—accuracy is determined, *not* by you, but by the link that receives the information you pass on. Up or down. There is one simple, critical rule right here, particularly applicable in the tricky business of moving *orders* downward. *Always* check to see that an order is understood. An affirmative nod or a "Roger" on the radio is often not enough. When there's time, and you're moving a critical order, ask the link on the receiving end to say back the information you sent. And further, if you're good, you won't quit there. You'll watch to see what *happens* as a result of the information you sent.

To discuss these three things (get, process, and move information) that you do as a link in a chain of command communicating in battle, we had to slow down the action. And we had to break down a highly complex, high-speed activity so you could better understand what the chain of command is and how it functions. But it's never that clean and neat and simple. Go back to Chapter 1, to young Stan Goff and that day when he and "the pig" brought so much misery to the enemy. Think about the things Stan did from the time the action started until it ended. Stan was at the end of the chain of command. The courage in that action was Stan's, but a chain of command was providing the coordination and control. Think about each of the small-unit level links—the squad leader, platoon leader, company commander—and the kinds of information that had to be moving up and down. Watch a chain of command at work—in battle. All that we have discussed is there, boiled down to the basics.

Those same basics apply today, right now, as our Army prepares for war, as it always does in peacetime. The chain of command coordinates and controls; orders and planning information flow down; reports and requests flow up; and each link in the chain *gets, processes,* and *moves* information. But the day-to-day activities of an Army preparing for war are far more complex. *Fighting* the battle takes only a short time. *Getting ready* to fight is a full-time, long-term, everyday activity with a multitude of tasks to be accomplished. And right here is the best place to bring in another leadership mechanism closely related to the chain of command.

THE NCO SUPPORT CHANNEL

In the early part of this chapter, we talked about the company—169 men. Of those 169 men, 49 are officers and 120 are not. Of those 49 officers, 6 are commissioned and 43 are not. Credentials and insignia establish a difference between the two kinds of officers, but the more important difference is that they do different things and have different *responsibilities.* When this difference is clearly understood and then applied, our Army gets more of the same kind of "extra" we saw back in Chapter 2, where recognition of the differences between levels of leadership kept leaders from getting into each other's business.

The same thing applies to understanding and *using* the difference between officers and NCOs. If this difference is not understood and put to work, there is no way the *unit* can accomplish all the tasks necessary in the day-to-day business of preparing for war. The purpose of this whole chapter has been to help you figure out what are the right things to do and how to get them done. An understanding of this difference we are about to explain is absolutely essential to both tasks.

For years, Army leaders in the Motor Pool, the Mess Hall, and the XO's office talked about an informal "NCO Chain of Command." There is no such thing. There is only one chain of command in our Army, and it's composed of officers *and* NCOs. What these leaders were talking about was an informal NCO channel of information and support that paralleled and reinforced the formal chain of command. The difference between these two leadership mechanisms was never clarified or taught in our leadership schools or officially recognized. Not until late in 1976.

At that time, two first sergeants and a leadership instructor sat down and wrote a short fifty-page Army field manual called *The Army Non-Commissioned Officer Guide.* In that manual, they explained what is now known formally as "the NCO support channel." They also spelled out clearly the differences between the duties and responsibilities of officers and NCOs and described how these differences are put to work through the mutual support of the chain of command *and* the NCO support channel. This manual is neither "good to know" nor "nice to know." At small-unit level, in any kind of unit, it is flat-out, downright, absolutely essential —for NCOs *and,* maybe even more so, for officers.

As you try to figure out what to do and how to get it done, whether you're an officer or an NCO, know that there are some basic differences between what officers do and what NCOs do in accomplishing the multitude of tasks required in an Army getting ready to fight. The six points below spell out this special officer/NCO relationship. If *both* officers and NCOs understand this relationship and make it work, the *unit* gets an "extra."

OFFICER	NONCOMMISSIONED OFFICER
The officer commands, establishes policy, plans and programs the work of the Army.	The NCO conducts the daily business of the Army within established orders, directives, and policies.
The officer concentrates on collective training which will enable the unit to accomplish its mission.	The NCO concentrates on individual training which develops the capability to accomplish the mission.
The officer is primarily involved with unit operations, training, and related activities.	The NCO is primarily involved with training individual soldiers and teams.
The officer concentrates on unit effectiveness and unit readiness.	The NCO concentrates on each subordinate NCO and soldier and on the small teams of the unit—to insure that each of them is well trained, highly motivated, ready, and functioning.
The officer pays particular attention to the standards of performance, training, and professional development of officers and NCOs.	The NCO concentrates on standards of performance, training, and professional development of NCOs and young soldiers.
The officer creates conditions —makes the time and other resources available—so the NCO can do the job.	The NCO gets the job done.

100 TASKS, COMPETING DEMANDS, AND SHIFTING PRIORITIES

At 1215 on the sixth of February 1980, an informal study was made of what was going on inside the "brain" of a randomly selected U.S. Army rifle company. This unit was in its training phase—preparing for war. In about a month, it was due to move out on a major FTX. It was a good solid average rifle company.

The "study" of what the unit was doing was made simply by making a list of what was on the desktops of the CO, the XO, and the First Sergeant. In-boxes, out-boxes, notebooks, scraps of paper, official correspondence, and forms. The inventory is as follows:

1. Note to turn in cash collection sheet to Bn Mess Hall
2. Computer printout of unit equipment from Computerized Movement and Planning System (COMPASS)
3. AR on Assignment of Personnel with Handicapped Dependents
4. Receipt for $19.60 for attendance of LT & Mrs. Greene at a battalion function
5. CBR Officer Course certificate to be given to LT Lewis
6. FM on organizational maintenance operations
7. Draft EER for M. Sgt. Stack
8. Forms, statements, and reports pertaining to theft of $100 bill
9. Note from Bn, informing XO he would be appointed investigating officer for above
10. Note to XO to round up references (FMs, SOPs, OPlans) for FTX
11. Letter from Bn: Buck up performance of officers appointed as Report of Survey Officer, 3-page checklist attached
12. Penciled list of FTX Preparation Actions:
    07 Feb: Bde Chem Officer to check company CBR teams
    07 Feb: Briefings for dependents on FTX
    07 Feb: Bde practice convoy for FTX
    11–13 Feb: Bde FTX
    11–17 Feb: Bn FM radio update
    15 Feb: FTX convoy briefings
    19 Feb: FTX Advance Party depart
    21 Feb: Submit FTX rail movement data
    25 Feb: Bn wheeled convoy departs for FTX
    28 Feb: Submit FTX air movement data
    04 Mar: Bde Communications Exercise
    07–13 Mar: FTX

20–21 Mar: Rail deployment, FTX return

22–25 Mar: Air deployment, FTX return

24–28 Mar: Wheel deployment, FTX return

13. Note to put concertina around Motor Pool parking lot (Sister Bn has AGI)

14. DF from Bn: Staff Duty Officer roster

15. DF from Bn: LT Lewis go for Officer Record Brief

16. Bn SOP on reports

17. EER for Mess Sgt

18. Hand receipt for Mess equipment used to feed mortar section in the field

19. Claim form against soldier who kicked window out of private car

20. Ammo request for mortar training

21. DF from Bn: Training notes on "lessons learned"

22. Ltr from member of unit who had PCS'd 3 months earlier

23. Range request for mortar training

24. Hand receipt for 1 folding cot

25. Bar to reenlistment form for PVT in the unit

26. DF from Bn: Complete OER support forms

27. Article 15 Record of Proceedings on PFC who failed to go to field training

28. Weekly training schedule

29. Note to counsel Smith, Jones, and Harris on reenlistment

30. Equipment Dispatch Annex to Bn Maintenance SOP

31. Set of handbooks for "PEGASUS" CPX

32. DF on suspension of Art. 15 punishment for Specialist Hammond

33. DF from Bn: Submit handwritten training schedule

34. EER for SSG Moon

35. Diagrams for combat loading of vehicles

36. Separate ration authorization for PFC Richards

37. Medical examination report on little finger of PFC Atkins, with note from Bn to complete Line of Duty investigation NLT 15 February

38. 1st Platoon loading plans

39. Ltr from Bn: Composition of FTX Advance Party

40. List of junior NCOs to attend Bn Leader Development program

41. Ltr from Div: TOW and DRAGON training

42. DA Circular on SQT for FY 1980

43. Ft. Benning text: Plt. Ldr. Training Management Planning Book

44. Training Circular on tank-mech infantry team

45. Battalion ARTEP

46. Ft. Benning text: Infantry Co. Cmdr.'s Handbook
47. List of men absent from PT
48. Schedule of reenlistment interviews
49. DF from Bn: Soldier of the Month
50. DF from Bn: Motor Pool Police Responsibilities
51. DF from Bn: Staff Duty NCO Roster
52. DF from Bn: Regional Marksmanship Championships
53. List of personnel requiring yellow fever shots
54. DF from medic: Names of men due overweight weigh-in checks
55. DF on individuals to attend remedial PT on Saturday
56. DF for LT Greene to take annual medical exam
57. DF from Bn: School quotas
58. Sick slip for PVT Flores: with sprained ankle
59. Sick slip for PVT Barder: with lung trouble
60. Academic report on E–5 who completed BNCOC
61. DF from Bn: Appointment of E–5/E–6 Promotion Board
62. PT Scorecard for Specialist Jenkins
63. DF listing authorized SD assignments
64. DF listing marksmanship scores of all individuals in unit
65. Request for school allocations
66. Computer printout of unit SQT Report
67. Request for quota to bus-driving school
68. Notes from 1 meeting of "Things to Do" before FTX

   (1) Load sensitive items at Bldg. 311
   (2) Put out emergency leave procedure to all troops
   (3) Submit Rear Detachment list to Bn NLT Monday, 1200
   (4) Leave extra keys for Rear Detachment
   (5) Send 1 NCO and 2 men to railhead for loading
   (6) Send troops to cold weather classes on 15 Feb
   (7) Submit POV list to Bn Tuesday
   (8) Advance party: take 1 CONEX (with rifle racks) per Co
   (9) Send 2 men to Bn S2 for LRRP
   (10) Submit report on Reports of Survey, prior to FTX
   (11) Mark all individual duffle bags prior to FTX (Red)
   (12) XO check drive-trains of all vehicles
   (13) Claims officer to brief troops Monday
   (14) Bring enough trash bags for whole exercise
   (15) Issue luminous tape for all troops
   (16) Send drivers to Bn for XO maintenance class, 1400

Now let's first talk about that whole list for a moment, then move to the point where *you* get involved in that lash-up, and then work out some more how-to's to help you figure out what to do and get it done.

That list is only a stop-action snapshot of *some* of the things going on in a unit at a specific moment in time. It is nowhere near complete. First and foremost, it does not include all the individual training that's going on all the time. When the "thing" fights, you remember, it needs fifteen hundred individual skills. The school system itself only gives the soldiers about 50 to 60 percent of these. The rest are the responsibility of the *unit,* developed in the unit, day to day, on the job. And, as you saw a few pages ago, the NCOs in the unit are responsible for getting this done.

Nor does the list include what came down yesterday, and the day before that. Or what's coming tomorrow, and the day after that. And the list only includes what's written down. It doesn't include all the "things to do" that are not written down but are in the *minds* of the CO, XO, and First Sergeant. Nor does it include the "things to do" that these men have figured out for themselves without being told by the next higher headquarters. Nor does it include what's coming in over the telephone which, according to the "study," rings just about once every 7.5 minutes, usually bringing down more "things to do."

The brain of the company is a *busy* place, simply because, more than any other headquarters in our Army, it is on the receiving end of all the "what-to-do's" and "how-to-get-it-done's" flowing downward through the chain from every one of those levels of leadership up above the captains.

If you took all the tasks on that close to 100-item list and added to that all the tasks in the minds and notebooks of those three men and added to that all that's in the minds and notebooks of the rest of the lieutenants and sergeants, your list of what the unit does on an average day of getting ready for war would be in the thousands. How do all those tasks get done? The first words in this book pointed the way: those thousands of tasks get done by **THE LEADERSHIP.**

Now, back to the Orderly room and that written-down list. How to unscramble who does what? It's relatively simple. The First Sergeant's there, and he'll take at least half of these items and get them moving over in the NCO support channel. Those items are "sergeants' business," and, when you learn what's in that basic NCO manual we mentioned earlier, you'll know which items fit in this category. The CO and the XO will take the rest of the items and get them moving through the chain of command. The XO will handle mostly the administrative, supply, and maintenance tasks; and the CO will mainly ride herd on the training. The CO will work with the lieutenants; the lieutenants and the First Sergeant will work with NCOs; the NCOs will work with the soldiers; and the soldiers will *do* the work.

This is the basic process by which the *unit* gets things done—all those things on that list and all those other things not written down. This process will occur, just about as described, when the leadership of the unit has developed the "vertical teamwork" we have mentioned before. And "vertical teamwork" is built by *THE LEADERSHIP* accomplishing four things: knowing each other; practicing this basic process together; knowing how the chain of command and the NCO support channel work; and knowing the differences between what officers do and what NCOs do. The whole process is pretty simple. And best of all, it *works*.

You—Captain, Lieutenant, or Sergeant—fit somewhere in this process. Of those thousands of tasks to be accomplished by the leadership of the unit, you will get your fair share—plus some other things that you yourself think need to get done. Let's say you've got a hundred. Big, and little. Hard, and easy. Nasty, and nice. And never enough time. Now how do you work out a game plan for "what to do?" Again, it's fairly simple, and there are some basic how-to's that will help.

What you're trying to do at this point is begin to develop a "sense of priority." What's *important* and *why*. If you can get a good handle on this, then take your list of "things to do" and give each one a number, from No. 1 (Hot) all the way down to 100. Next, take the amount of effort you have available—yours and your soldiers'—and start allocating to each task enough effort to get the job done to the *standards* established. Keep parceling out effort down the list until you run out. Maybe you get down to about No. 85. At this point, you still have fifteen things to do, but you don't have any more effort to allocate. Don't quit!

Go back and look at the standards of the tasks you've already planned to put effort into. Have you allocated extra effort to some of them so that you can get them done to *above* standards? That sounds nice, and is a good idea, *when* you have time and effort to spare. But you don't. You've still got fifteen things to do, and you've flat run out of effort. Forget about the *above* standards business. A dozen things done "good" is far better than two things done "best" and ten things done "sorry." Plan to achieve *established* standards. What that does is give you some more effort to allocate to those tasks still remaining there at the bottom of the list. Allocate that extra effort you just found and you cover maybe five more of the fifteen. Don't quit. Hang in there.

You still have ten more tasks to go. Now, all along, you've probably been holding out a little reserve effort. Look at the last ten items on your list, then think about your reserve. You may have hit that reserve pretty hard yesterday, or you may need it tomorrow for more important things.

So at this point, put some of that reserve on two or three more of those last ten tasks. Then quit. Just gamble. Take the risk. And hope that the last seven or eight tasks will get done by themselves. They probably will.

What we have discussed here, in an exaggerated example, is the way a leader *budgets and organizes effort*—his own and that of his soldiers. Seldom is it done in the precise step-by-step way we have described. It is, like other basics we have discussed, a thought process, a way of thinking, another thing that in time must become instinctive—automatic.

None of this budgeting of effort can occur without the "sense of priority" we mentioned at first. There are at least four or five good ways to develop this sense.

Take your hundred tasks and go back to the "Golden Rule" we discussed earlier in this chapter. Which ones of the hundred are most closely related to the two basic responsibilities of captains, lieutenants, and sergeants? The answer won't tell you that you can ignore any of the hundred, but it will give you the big picture of what's important. Everything related to training, for example, will start to stand out as more important.

What's your mission? Not the big overall mission like "fight and win the land battle," but the two or three main objectives that the next higher link has laid out for you for the next few months. Like maybe, "support post details in January; train for the FTX in February; pass the AGI in March." You have to know these things. And if your leader hasn't laid them on you, then just *ask* him. Once you know what these missions are, get out your list of tasks. Now, which ones are absolutely essential to accomplishing your mission? In other words, if these tasks aren't done, there's no way the mission can be accomplished. Identify those tasks. They are mission *needs*. The tasks that remain are *wants*—yours or someone else's. You still can't throw out any tasks, but now you're starting to get a handle on "what's important." And, in this case, "mission" was the tool you started with.

What are *your* priorities? Well, after the two techniques just discussed, you've got some idea now, but you don't run the whole show. What about the next link up in the chain of command? What are *his* priorities? He's probably got four or five. They represent *some* of what he thinks is most important, but mostly, they represent what *his* leader thinks is most important. That's because *he* doesn't run the whole show either. And neither does *his* leader. The point here is that *the chain of command* is what carries the priorities in a unit. Why is that? So that leaders can budget effort. The NCO support channel, if it's tuned right, will carry the same priorities and budget effort—not up and down every day or so, but as major changes occur in "the situation." One primary thing that the chain of command and the NCO support channel do—together—is keep the whole unit aware of these changing priorities *and* the reasons why they're changing.

Now back to your leader. What are his four or five priorities? If he hasn't spelled them out for you, then, *ask* him. And then ask him something else. *Ask* him to put a priority on the priorities. Rank order, 1–5. This won't make him mad. Guaranteed. He probably thinks you already know, but he's been too busy to check. And he is as interested as you are in getting the effort budget balanced. He also has 100 items on *his* list.

Finally, if changes and more tasks are beginning to pile up and get ahead of you, sit down and write down a list of *all* the tasks that seem to be "No. 1." Take it to your leader, and *ask* him for help in getting it sorted out into at least three categories: *important, MORE important, MOST important.* Again, he won't mind. Keeping priorities straight is a most important part of the definition of leadership. Like you, he wants to get the *right* things done. And, if he's smart, he might add a fourth category: "Things that are most important whether you and I think they are or not, but which we are going to get *done.*"

In most of this discussion of developing a "sense of priority," we have pointed you toward the chain of command—to your leader and to what he is supposed to do in the priority business. A main responsibility of your leader is to set priorities for you, the follower. Now think about this a minute; this also tells you what *your* responsibilities are to the next link down in the chain of command. To *your* followers.

The *sense of priority* and the *budgeting of effort* are important basics in the techniques of how to lead. Without both, there will *always* be confusion and wasted effort down through the levels of the unit. In peacetime, this results in situations where leaders get their heels locked, or where soldiers "hurry up and wait." On the battlefield, where priorities are unclear and effort is wasted, then leaders and soldiers and units die —and lose.

This has been a long chapter, full of basics about how to figure out the right things to do and get them done. We saw that the "unit" is a *whole* thing, composed of parts put together, and how it is not any individual leader, not even the company commander, but *the leadership* of the unit that puts it together. All of it, from company commander to fire-team leader. You saw the insides of the chain of command and learned its language, built around TROOP-LEADING PROCESS, THE ESTIMATE OF THE SITUATION, and THE FIVE-PARAGRAPH FIELD ORDER. All these basics work, not only in times of war, but in times of preparing for war as well. We discussed a new leadership mechanism, the NCO support channel, put together by our NCO Corps to help Army leadership do a better job of getting the right things done right. Finally, we saw a company today working hard at the many tasks required of an Army getting ready to fight, and you learned that a sense of mission and an understanding of priority must be behind all that our Army does. Nowhere is that better said than in the "Golden Rule."

So we have come full circle, the primary objective of our Army is *to win the land battle.* In support of this objective, captains, lieutenants, and sergeants have two basic responsibilities:

- LEADING SOLDIERS AND SMALL UNITS DURING BATTLE
- PREPARING SOLDIERS AND SMALL UNITS TO FIGHT THE BATTLE

How to Develop Soldiers

LEADERSHIP ARITHMETIC

Throughout this book, we have emphasized the fact that what wins on the battlefield is *skill, will,* and *teamwork.* Another way of saying this is that how well a UNIT does depends upon a basic "formula" of leadership arithmetic. This first formula says:

> The sum of the performances of the individual soldiers × the ability of the soldiers to work together as a team × the ability of the leadership to get all those teams to work together as a unit = THE PERFORMANCE OF A UNIT.

This formula shows clearly that the fundamental building block of unit performance is the performance of the individual soldier. And just as there is a basic leadership formula for unit performance, there is another for INDIVIDUAL performance. The second formula says:

> The soldier's skill in performing tasks critical to success on the battlefield × his will to learn and put that skill to work = THE PERFORMANCE OF THE INDIVIDUAL SOLDIER.

Here in Chapter 4, we will concentrate on how to develop the *skill* and the *will* of the soldier. Then, in Chapter 5, we will focus specifically on the third critical factor, *teamwork,* and lay out techniques for how to build teamwork in the unit.

SKILL AND WILL

In developing soldiers, the leadership of the unit must build skill *and* will. Either one without the other is admirable, but by itself, it won't win. The marksmanship skills of an expert rifleman are officially recognized as "outstanding." The rifleman is rewarded with a special medal. Years ago, he got extra pay. But all that skill is precisely worthless if in battle he is not willing to take the risk, stick his head up, and kill somebody. And all that skill is also worthless if as he takes aim his weapon won't fire because he has not been willing to keep it maintained and ready, especially on those cold, rainy, muddy winter nights when his fingers were numb and blue.

So on the other hand, will without skill is also worthless. If our rifleman has little skill as a marksman but is willing to assault the enemy, swinging his weapon like a club, that's very heroic. But if the enemy meets all this fine will with one well-aimed shot, our man loses. High levels of will can often compensate for lower levels of skill, and vice versa. However, soldiers who are best prepared to fight have high levels of *both.*

It should be obvious to you now that skill and will are linked together. Each affects the other. When we first discussed the prime standard for your leadership, we said that, on the battlefield, the prime standard centers around the *confidence* of the soldier. And the soldier's confidence is, very simply, based on a combination of his skill and his will. Therefore, if the leadership of the unit is to meet the prime standard of leadership, then it must build *both.*

BUILDING SKILL

Building skill is, simply, training. But that simple word is all-important. The "Golden Rule" that we've discussed before tells you that if you're not leading on the battlefield right now you should be *preparing soldiers and small units to fight the battle.* Furthermore, that simple word "training" isn't all that simple.

If you rounded up all the training manuals for a rifle company, for example, you'd find that all the different jobs in a company require a total of about fifteen hundred individual skills. These individual skills, in various combinations, must be put together for the performance of more than five hundred collective skills. In the company, all that adds up to over two thousand different items of skill.

As captain, lieutenant, or sergeant, you are personally *responsible* for some portion of that 2,000-item list. Did you ever sit down, round up the appropriate Soldier's Manuals and ARTEPS, and do an "inventory" of the items on your part of the list? You do that for the property and equipment you've signed for. And when you're short items on your equipment list, you pay out of your pocket. Now who is it that's going to pay for the shortages on your training list? With what? When and where? Figure this out and you'll see that right now you ought to be giving some serious thought to inventorying your training list and getting to work on the shortages. The title "NCO" or "officer" says that you are "signed for" the skills of your men and your unit. The *big* inventory will come—on the battlefield.

Two thousand training tasks. How does the leadership of the unit handle all that? You already know. Remember the basic tools of leadership we used to tackle that list of "100 things to do" in Chapter 3? Those tools worked for handling those hundred items coming over the desktops. They'll work just as well for handling the two thousand items on the training list—for building the skills for which the leadership of the unit is responsible, and which the unit needs to fight.

The ESTIMATE, the TROOP-LEADING PROCESS, and the FIVE-PARAGRAPH FIELD ORDER give you all you need to analyze the problems of individual and collective training and get the orders and instructions moving. You're going to have to develop a "sense of priority," too. What priority will *training* have in the unit? And then, among the skill shortages on that 2,000-item training list, which ones are important, MORE important, and MOST important? Knowing this, you and the rest of the leadership of the unit are then going to have to budget and organize the effort that's going to be put into training. Finally, just as we found when we tackled the "100 things to do," *the key factor* in handling the 2,000-item training list is knowing the difference between what officers do and what NCOs do.

INDIVIDUAL AND COLLECTIVE TRAINING

About one-fourth of those two thousand skills are collective training. The remaining fifteen hundred are individual training. Training time for collective training will usually be scheduled formally on the unit training schedule. Individual training won't be, as a rule. Individual training must be integrated with other activities. When it's done right, it's done right along with collective training. It's done during breaks. It's done on the job. It's done when changes provide a little extra time. It's done whenever soldiers run into those "hurry-up-and-wait" situations. Individual training is done all the time, right along with everything else. Out in the field, and down in the Motor Pool. Integrated. Concurrent. Preplanned. Executed. And checked.

While individual training doesn't get the special attention that collective training does, it is, nevertheless, the flat-out MOST important of the two types. We said earlier that individual skills were the fundamental building blocks underlying the performance of the unit. Collective skills are *dependent* on individual skills. A squad live-fire exercise is nothing but a worthless, deadly waste of time if the soldiers don't have the individual skills required to aim and fire their weapons properly. Individual skills, the building blocks of the foundation, have *got* to come first, THE top priority.

WHO DOES WHAT

Individual training is sergeants' business. Officers focus more on collective training. The officers' job is to take the individual skills that the NCOs have developed, put them together in such a way as to accomplish collective tasks or missions, and ensure that *unit* training standards are met. The officers, however, cannot concentrate solely on collective skills, just as the NCO cannot concentrate solely on individual skills. The lieutenant is as surely responsible for the ability of his men to mask in nine seconds as the sergeant is responsible for the performance of his squad *as a team* in the "Forced March, Live Fire" mission of the ARTEP.

For a good handle on who does what in individual and collective training, go back for a minute to Chapter 3 and look at the differences between what officers do and what NCOs do. You'll see there a clear breakout of training responsibilities in the all-important business of developing soldiers.

The NCOs lead the way in the business of developing individual skill. Individual training is MOST important: there's far more of it to do, it's going on all the time, and collective training depends on it. That's why the NCO is called "the backbone of our Army." That's why we said earlier that training is "sergeants' business." That being the case, then, it's easy to see that the head sergeant in the unit has to be the head trainer: the First Sergeant. The First Sergeant can't possibly accomplish all that individual training by himself. His training job is to see that the individual training *gets accomplished.* He does this by analyzing, organizing, deputizing, and supervising within his NCO support channel. The First Sergeant is in this respect the chief "training manager" for *individual* training in the unit. This makes the First Sergeant responsible for about three-fourths of those two thousand items and for making up the shortages. In a full strength unit, he has forty-two other NCOs to help him *get the job done.* Let's look a little more closely at this particular kind of "sergeants' business."

WHAT'S MOST IMPORTANT

What is the "most important" critical task for an 11B rifleman? Is it to qualify with the M–16? Know how to stop the bleeding? Maintain physical fitness? Or one of the other 287 individual skills that a rifleman must know to give him the best chance to win on the battlefield?

To figure out what's most important in building the soldier's skill, and to get that skill built, you have three things to do, Sergeant, as a bare minimum. First, it is a fact that you, as a leader, have some part of that 2,000-item skill list as your *personal* responsibility. So right off the bat, you need to know the individual skills that you're responsible for developing, and you need to know what your shortages are. What Smith is short, what Brown is short, and right on down the line. You need to know who is short what skills and work on the *shortages.* It doesn't make much sense to waste time and effort training in skills that a subordinate already has. Years ago, we used to do that. We don't now.

Next, you have to look at your shortages and work out a sense of priority for making them up. Since time is always scarce, it makes good sense to make up the MOST important shortages first. What's most important depends on at least six factors:

1. The tactical mission of the unit
2. The geographical area where the unit is stationed
3. The type of terrain
4. The capabilities of the enemy
5. The training priorities coming down through the NCO support channel
6. The individual skills scheduled for testing on the next SQT

Further, if you *really* want to get a good handle on your priorities, evaluate each individual skill shortage in terms of who else is going to be affected by that shortage and what that effect might be. For example, how about the individual skill shortages of one of the mechanics down in the Motor Pool?

Finally, once you know what your shortages are and which of those shortages are most important, then you need to work out a plan—a concept of operation—for making up what you're short. When are you going to train who how to do what? When you've got that figured out, you take these three things (shortages, priorities, plan) and check them out with the next higher level in the NCO support channel. When you have this all coordinated, you get hold of Smith and Brown and execute the last two steps of the TROOP-LEADING PROCESS: *issue orders* and *supervise.*

None of this is as complicated as it may seem. It's sergeants' business, and in a well-trained unit it's routine, normal, and natural. This particular kind of TROOP-LEADING PROCESS will take some thinking on your part, a little work in the Soldiers' Manuals, a couple of pages in your notebook, and maybe a little time with other NCOs in the Mess Hall.

ALL THE TIME, EVERY DAY, ANYWHERE

Building skill is simply training, but not the kind of training you usually find in a school or a classroom or blocked out on a training schedule. In building individual skills in individual soldiers, *any* time that you explain or show a subordinate how to do a task, then have him do it, then tell him what he's doing right and wrong—that's training. *Any* time you give an order, then supervise, then check completion against standards—that's training, too. Maybe not skill training, but certainly training in "how to" do two critical things: follow instructions and obey orders.

The point to remember here is that a good leader should be training, building skill, and developing soldiers *all* the time, not just during "scheduled training." And it must be that way. Fifteen hundred different individual skills are what that "thing" that we talked about needs when it fights on the battlefield. The school system only provides about one-half to two-thirds of these individual skills. The rest are developed in the unit by the leadership of the unit, primarily by the First Sergeant, his NCOs, and the NCO support channel. If the sergeants doing sergeants' business don't make up the shortages in individual skills, the efforts of the officers to develop collective *unit* skills are nothing but "show" and wasted effort, resulting in bored troops and an unready unit. What is required is "vertical teamwork" of the highest order. Never before has the NCO Corps had such a clear-cut and awesome responsibility.

As we wind up this section on BUILDING SKILL, here are a few questions for you, Sergeant. The eighth principle of leadership holds you responsible to develop your subordinates. Who are your immediate subordinates right now? Think about each one of them—Smith, Brown, and all the rest. How does each man look in terms of skill shortages? What's your plan for developing the skills of each one of those men? And who's going to pay for the shortages if you don't make them up? Where and when?

BUILDING WILL

"Will," in our terms, is something like "morale." But "morale" doesn't say enough about determination. "Determination," by itself, doesn't say enough, either. Determination to do what? Determination to fight. That's getting better, but it's still not enough. Determination to fight and win? That's good, and now we've worked our way up to "will to win." But we're *still* not on target. Almost every man has the will to win when he fights, especially on the battlefield. It's something "built-in" in the human species. Building the will to win isn't hard. What *is* hard to build is the will *to work to get ready to win.* That critical element of will is what makes champion athletes. It's also what makes champion soldiers. How do you build that kind of will?

A straight answer to almost anything in the complex business of leadership is usually hard to find, but in this case, there *is* one best way to build in the soldier the kind of will we've said we need. It doesn't involve any complex "motivation analysis" or require any special training program for leaders, and it works for virtually all soldiers across the board. Furthermore, you already know how to do it! The one best way to build will is to build skill. By *training.*

The key to building WILL is building SKILL. The proof that this is a *fact* is overwhelming.

The main evidence comes from over a thousand scientific studies of what makes men satisfied with their work. The notion was that men who were more satisfied, or "happier," would be more productive. The thousand studies *dis*proved this notion! What the research said instead was that productivity will lead to satisfaction far more often than satisfaction will lead to productivity. "Productivity" in a unit preparing for war means *training.* So what those thousand studies say, when translated into Army language, is that if you're concerned about building skill and will, the best place to start working is with skill. SKILL is the key to WILL. That's what the research flat-out *proves.*

The wisdom of experience tells you the same thing. Watch what happens when a unit starts having an increasing number of "will" problems—AWOLs, Article 15's, larcenies, all on the rise. What you'll see when that happens is that the old, wise, experienced leaders start jockeying schedules and requirements around so that they can get the soldiers out into the field to train. The more the unit and its soldiers *train,* the more the "will" problems disappear.

Soldiers want to train. It is training more than anything else that gives a soldier "job satisfaction," makes him "happy," determines his "quality of life." Ever notice young soldiers who have just completed Basic Training? Will, morale, appearance, attitude, and enthusiasm are at a peak. Why is that? It's because Basic Training is almost all *training.* "Soldier" training.

Soldiers want to train. Sit down with a few in the Mess Hall and talk with 'em sometime. In their time-honored tradition, they'll complain about training just as they do about leaders, but deep down inside, you'll find they want to train, to learn soldier skills, to *work to get ready to win.* Why is this so? Because they know that that's what *soldiers* are supposed to do. They know that's what their nation, their families, other soldiers, their leaders, and people in general *expect* them to do. They want to train so they can know their effort is going toward something "worthwhile." And they want to train well, so they can see themselves as "winners."

ABLE AND WILLING

To summarize, developing soldiers means building skill *and* will. You know that building skill, training, is the primary task and principal responsibility for any company-level leader this side of the battlefield. We have discussed some of the how-to's of training at small-unit level, focusing mostly on individual training. Finally, in the preceding section, we laid out proof that the one best way to build will is to build skill. All this points out "how to" develop soldiers in general. But every soldier is a different individual, and what you need now are some how-to's for developing *individual* soldiers. What works well for building skill and will in one soldier may not work at all for the next. Soldiers aren't machines.

The standard for you in the task of developing soldiers is to produce a man who is both able and willing. Some soldiers are able and willing all the time. They have the skill and the will, no matter what task you give them. Some have the will; they try hard—but not the skill; whatever they touch turns to mud. Others have the ability to do the task you give them —but not the will; you have to stand over them and flat-out *make* them do the task.

What all the above means is that if you want to develop soldiers as *individuals,* then start by sizing up each soldier in terms of "HOW ABLE IS HE? and HOW WILLING IS HE?" Make an estimate. Check his head-space with an "able and willing" gauge. This simple basic estimate *works,* saves you time, helps you do the right things, and is, in addition to all that, logical. It makes good sense for a leader to come down hard on a soldier who has the ability to do a task but won't do it. On the other hand, it makes no sense at all to come down hard on a man who is trying his very best but has never been taught the skills required to do the task.

Knowing how to judge a soldier in terms of "able and willing" is the first step in developing soldiers *as individuals.* In the lists that follow are some ballpark traits and characteristics of soldiers in each of the four different categories of "able and willing." As you study these, think about your immediate subordinates, as individuals. Very few individuals will fit clearly and completely in any one category. But if you'll think about your man, you'll see that one of those four categories seems to describe him better than the others. In which category would Smith fit best? And Jones? And so on down the line. If you *know* your man, as the sixth principle of leadership requires, you'll get the right man in the right category about 90 percent of the time.

1. ABLE AND WILLING

- Has done the task right before
- Does many other tasks without being told
- Never seems satisfied until work is done "right"
- Accepts the need to put in extra time when necessary to get the job done
- Works out ways to get the job done better
- Recent performance has been satisfactory

2. UNABLE BUT WILLING

- Has never performed task before, or can't recall if he did
- Recent performance has been enthusiastic, particularly on tasks similar to what you want him to do now
- Pays close attention to your instruction
- Watches others doing same task; asks questions
- Spends some of his own time learning or practicing

3. ABLE BUT UNWILLING

- Recent performance has been off and on—sometimes to standard, sometimes below standard
- Has done the job right before, but keeps asking for instructions and assistance

- Doesn't appear to be concentrating—work is sporadic, poorly planned
- Takes every opportunity to be absent from training
- Lacks confidence in himself and his work

4. UNABLE AND UNWILLING

- Has never performed the task to standard before
- Recent performance has been below standard, even when he has received a lot of assistance and instruction
- Works only when closely supervised
- Seems satisfied with below-standard results
- Pays little attention to instructions; half-listens

The descriptors for each of the four categories above are only rough indicators. And the individual soldier may shift around from category to category, depending on the task and the effectiveness of your leadership. The point to remember is that each individual is different. And the differences that are most important to you in developing soldiers are the differences in skill and will. The ability to judge a subordinate on how well he measures up on both sides of the "able and willing" scale is another one of those basics that you must learn, practice, think about, and turn into instinct. Soldiers aren't machines. They are men, each one different from the other. A big part of your job is knowing those differences, then using that knowledge to lead better and smarter.

A soldier who is fully **"able and willing"** is the living standard for you in the task of developing soldiers. You work with this man as if you were a **coach** with a good quarterback. He can operate with mission-type orders. He does the right thing, should *not* be given close supervision. What this soldier does best is get *your* job done and save *your* time. He earns *your* trust. This is the kind of man you want to start "grooming" for leadership. Finally, if you want to do the tricky business of "delegating" right, delegate important jobs *only* to the soldier you're sure is able and willing. The others will seldom get the job done.

The **"willing and unable"** soldier is the one who usually comes to you in the replacement stream. The new guy. You work with this man as if you were a **teacher.** There will be much that he doesn't know. The Army school system will have given him only maybe two-thirds of the skills that his MOS calls for. And he's probably never seen an operational "unit." These soldiers need careful handling. In all the confusion, these new men can become discouraged and frustrated very easily. They need patient instruction and a *lot* of feedback. They will eat up much of your time, but in this case, putting in the extra time is like putting money in the bank. Think back to that platoon sergeant in Vietnam who, even in the field on a combat mission, put in some extra time teaching Stan Goff how to work his magic with a machine gun.

The **"able but unwilling"** soldier is your main challenge. You know you have a good horse, and you take him to the water, but he just won't drink. You work with this man as if you were a **father.** His unwillingness may be only a lack of confidence. All he needs is a nudge, an opportunity, and some encouragement. Then again, this soldier might have a real problem—with a young wife, with a big debt, or with himself. The best thing you can do is let him tell you about it. *Listen* to him. Finally, the able but unwilling soldier may be getting over on you. Shirking. So, in either case—the man with the problem or the shirker—insist that he complete the task, and make him do it to standards. The man with the problem will feel he's done something worthwhile, and the shirker will learn that, with you, the "shirk" don't work.

The **"unable and unwilling"** soldier shouldn't be in your unit in the first place. Somewhere along the line, a poor leader knowingly let him in the Army, passed him on, or let him slip through. You work with this man as if you were a **warden.** He doesn't know how to do his job, and he doesn't care about learning. He is a "quitter." Instead of punishing him when he quits on you, *make him complete the task.* If you *punish* a quitter, then he is smarter than you are. If he doesn't want to do the job, and you punish him instead of making him do it, then he gets what he wanted. You think you punished him, but you really rewarded him. He outsmarted you.

Making the unable and unwilling soldier complete a task to standards has another advantage. Maybe you'll lead him to something he's never learned much about—success at some skill. And maybe that success at some skill will build a little more willingness. And he'll try another skill, and —there he goes! Finally, a turned-on soldier. Salvaged. That's nice, and you'll be able to salvage maybe one out of five, after you have invested more hours in those five men than in all of your other men put together. Putting a lot of time and effort on the unable and unwilling soldier is noble and humane. It is not, however, "leadership effective" in terms of the effort you must invest, the return our Army gets on that investment, the other things you have to do, and the other soldiers who would benefit far more from your time and effort. Don't pass this man on or let him slip through. There is no place for him on the battlefield when that "thing" we called a unit does its work. Get the paperwork started. Tomorrow.

In this section, we have given you a simple and accurate "how-to" for identifying four different categories of soldiers. The differences have nothing to do with race, creed, color, sex, or appearance. The differences have to do simply with SKILL and WILL, which is what you as a leader are responsible for developing in your soldiers. When you size up a soldier, you should be sizing him up on skill and will. Skill times **Will** equals Performance. Performance is what gets the task done. Remember the purpose of leadership?—to accomplish the task.

Since there are four different categories of soldiers, it stands to reason that there is probably a "best way" to lead each kind—a best "leadership strategy" for developing soldiers in each of the four categories. We have also discussed variations on the able and willing scale. We have discussed generally what each of these leadership strategies should be. The tactics that go with each of these strategies are spelled out in the four sections below. Study them. Use them. And ask the wise old leaders for the "tricks of the trade" that will make each strategy and tactic work *better.*

1. ABLE AND WILLING

   - Tell him *what* you want done. Don't waste time telling him *how.* He already knows.
   - Tell him when to get started and when to be finished.
   - Supervise easy. Let him work. Give him your trust.
   - *Always* tell this kind of soldier how well he met your standards.
   - Stretch him out with a little more responsibility each time.

2. UNABLE BUT WILLING

   - Tell him what you want done. Tell him why. Tell him how and show him how—and where and with what, and when to start, and when to finish.
   - Encourage him to ask questions.
   - *Show* him the standard. Demonstrate it if you can. Let him *see* what things look like when the job is done right.
   - Supervise closely. Check frequently. Help him correct mistakes. Give him time.
   - Reward heavy; punish easy.

3. ABLE BUT UNWILLING

   - Check first for *why* the soldier is unwilling. Probably one of two reasons: lack of confidence, or personal problem.
   - If he seems to lack confidence:

     Get him to tell you *how* he would do the task.

     Give him encouragement; get him started.

     Handle him as "able and willing."
   - If he appears to have a personal problem:

     Arrange for him to talk about it with you later. Give him a *specific* time.
   - Tell him what you want done, when to start, when to finish.

- Spell out clearly what the standards are.
- Spell out clearly what the reward or punishment will be.
- Supervise closely.
- Check task completion against standard.
- With this soldier, *always* follow through with the kind of reward or punishment you promised.

4. UNABLE AND UNWILLING

- Explain carefully *what* you want done and *how* you want him to do it.
- Question him to check that he knows exactly what to do.
- Spell out clearly what the standards are.
- Spell out clearly what the reward or punishment will be.
- Supervise *heavy;* this soldier will need frequent correction and will often quit working if he thinks he is not being watched.
- Check task completion against standards. Follow through with promised reward or punishment.
- If repeated efforts to help this soldier to become able or willing have failed, initiate action for unsuitability discharge. The few soldiers in this category, because they require detailed instructions and constant supervision, absorb enormous amounts of leader time and effort and are of little benefit to a unit preparing for war.

THE FIRST TEN DAYS

This side of the battlefield, there is no man in your crew, squad, platoon, or company who is more important than "the new guy" who just arrived. Why? Because he is the *future* of your unit. He is what will be there after you're gone—something to tell that leader who comes to replace you how good a leader you were. Furthermore, what you do with, to, and for that "new guy" in THE FIRST TEN DAYS will have a major impact on how well you get *your* tasks accomplished for as long as you remain in the unit.

THE FIRST TEN DAYS are critical. The scientists tell us that it takes a person about that long to get oriented to an entirely new situation and a new bunch of people. Think back to the last time you PCS'd. It probably took you about ten days to get the lay of the land. "What kind of an outfit is this? Do people seem to 'give a damn' about what they're doing, or not? Are they hard-core soldiers or wimps? What kind of leaders have we got? Which are good? Which are sorry? How's mine? Who knows the real skinny about what's happening around here? What are people going to expect of *me*? What are 'the rules of the game' about working and eat-ing and uniforms and formations and PT and barracks and off-duty time? What people around here will help me? Which ones do I like? Which ones can I trust? Which ones are going to be my buddies?"

These questions are pretty close to the ones that *you* were most concerned about the last time you were "the new guy." Where did you get your answers? You got some welcoming letters and routine "new guy" briefings, but most of your answers you got from people of about your own rank with whom you came in contact during your first ten days. And the answers to your questions came far more from informal, "grapevine" talk than from written-down, spelled-out formal policy and welcome letters. You were new and trying hard to get squared away, so you had all your antennae run out. Being the new guy is uncomfortable. Embarrassing. You wanted to "fit in" as soon as you could. You listened. Closely. Listened for what you thought were the "true" answers for each of your questions. Then, in a week or so, that was it—you got all your questions answered. You were "oriented."

The new guy, dragging that duffle bag, gets oriented the same way you did. Now, you can welcome him to the unit, run him through the chain, and let him sort of drift naturally through the first ten days, or knowing what's going to happen, you can put some knowledge of the "getting oriented" process to work to make your job of developing soldiers far more effective. You only have ten days. After that, it's normally too late. Here's why.

There are, in any unit, small groups of people who hang around together. Groups of buddies. Cliques. They *won't* usually parallel the organizational lines of the unit, and they *will* usually have a sort of natural, informal leader. Some of these groups are aimed toward the same objectives as the unit. They're good. A source of "extra" strength. Other groups aren't. They're aimed somewhere else, sometimes even against the objectives of the unit.

There are far more of the good groups than there are of the sorry groups, so the sorry groups, naturally, are always trying to gain more strength and power. Now, when you let the new guy just drift, guess who it is that's going to get to him first? Answer his questions and get him "oriented"? Your task as a leader is to get his questions answered *right.* IN THE FIRST TEN DAYS. After that, he's pretty much "locked in."

Give the new guy your extra effort and special attention. Assume right off the bat that he is "able and willing" or at least "willing but unable." Round up two of your own "able and willing" soldiers and lock 'em on the new guy like a leech for at least a week. Your able and willing soldiers are, as we said, your "living criteria," or standards, for what a good soldier should be. You want the new guy who's trying to get oriented to take his cues from them. You want your "able and willing" soldiers answering the new guy's questions and getting him moving into the "able and willing" informal groups. This does two things: it gets the new guy's orientation questions answered *right,* and just as important, it starts to dry up the sorry informal groups by wiping out their recruiting program. In time, therefore, you build a better future for your unit in *two* ways.

Thus far we have focused mostly on the new soldier coming right out of basic and advanced individual training, which is mostly "sergeants' business." But the same *general* principles will apply whether the new guy is a sergeant or a lieutenant—he will need close and special attention from an "able and willing," and from you. The FIRST TEN DAYS are critical and require the investment of extra effort on your part. Do the right things right, and you'll have more than double the return on your investment. Let him drift, and you're making more work for everyone.

The formal "Sponsorship Program" prescribed by regulations and memorandums gets the new guy *to* the unit. What happens after that, *in* the unit, is a leader's job, and you have to get it done in THE FIRST TEN DAYS.

DEVELOPING LEADERS

Find a bright orange grease pencil. At 1300 hours, after you've marched your squad or platoon down to the Motor Pool and got them going on the vehicles in preparation for next week's AGI, go find a jeep, parked in such a way that there isn't any glare on the windshield. With your grease pencil, write four bright orange words on the windshield, one under the other, in letters about an inch high:

```
ANALYZE
ORGANIZE
DEPUTIZE
SUPERVISE
```

Now go out among your soldiers and find an "able and willing," someone whom you've noticed has been pretty much the "main man" in one of those worthwhile hang-around-together buddy groups. Walk him back toward the jeep. If it's winter, and the jeep's been running, he'll gravitate naturally toward the hood. Point to those four words. And right there, at that moment, that man changes from an "able and willing" soldier to a "willing but unable" leader.

In no more than thirty minutes, there on the hood of the jeep, tell him what each of those words mean and what you know from experience about "how to" *do* each one. Task, conditions, standards. Then, don't just ask him if he understands. That never works very well. Get him to tell you how he would *do* each one. Spend a total of thirty minutes. Next, take him back to his crew or team and put him "in charge." Go about your business, but keep your eye on him. And on his men.

After you've marched your unit back to the company, and as you release them, fall out your young man. In no more than fifteen minutes, tell him how well he met your standards for each of these four words. What he did right and did wrong. Don't give him a lot of words about how to correct the wrongs. Instead, use the most powerful leadership tool you've got: set the example. Tell him to watch *you* for two or three days and to then be prepared to explain how *you* do it.

Next time down in the Motor Pool, or wherever, go ahead and get the unit to work, then fall the young man out again. Back to the jeep. In no more than ten minutes this time, have him tell you, now that he's watched *you* do it right, how he's going to do it. Then, back "in charge" again. Finally, at the end of the day, another five minutes for another critique. That's how to plant a leadership seed, in the total time of an hour, with one good soldier and a bright orange grease pencil. And you did it right along with everything else you've got to do.

Your investment was an hour's worth of time. What you did was take an able and willing soldier and get him started toward becoming an able and willing *leader*. Next week, he'll be closer to your standards. Then you can begin delegating to him some of the easy tasks at the bottom of your list of "100 things to do." That will save hours of *your* time. You get your time investment back, with interest. What do you do with the interest? Plow it right back in again. More teaching and coaching for the one you just got started, or plant some more seeds. Pretty soon, your young sprouts will become saplings, and you'll have a *performance*-based logic for telling you whom to promote, or get started up into the "pro" ranks of the NCO educational system.

There are about fifty officer positions in the unit. Some are filled by men coming in from outside, from schools and other units. *Most* are filled by men who start as leaders right there *in the unit*. That means that most of the leadership, for our whole Army, is started, planted, developed, by unit-level leaders, by you.

The simple Motor Pool example that we discussed is the essence of unit-level leadership development across the board. The example tells you that every "able and willing" soldier in your unit is a potential leader. And the example lays out a teaching technique that works, not just with young soldiers starting to become leaders, but with *any* leader who is able and willing—private, sergeant, or lieutenant. As *his* leader, part of your job is to keep him moving on up toward the next higher level. Coaching and critiquing will take your time. So will sending him to school. But the time isn't "spent." It is an *investment* and will come back to the leadership of your unit with interest.

Developing leaders, whether we're talking about starting new ones or "growing up" the ones who already have some experience, means *training* leaders. The best training strategy for developing *leadership skills* is the same one we discussed earlier for developing *individual skills.* The same principles apply. You have to do one of those "skill inventories." Just because he has stripes or bars doesn't mean he has all the leadership skills. Check him against the how-to's laid out in this book. What's he short? You will also have to find out how he stands on the "able and willing" scale. Just because he has stripes or bars doesn't automatically mean he's motivated.

Finally, just as with individual skills, the *time* for developing individual leadership skills won't often appear on the training schedule. It is done right along with everything else. Integrated. Concurrent. Preplanned. Executed. And checked. The bright orange grease pencil "training program" is a good example. Leader development goes on all the time. The Company Commander must have a *plan* for developing the lieutenants. The First Sergeant must have a *plan* for developing the NCOs.

Developing leaders means *training* leaders. Training means Task, Conditions, and Standards. How well *standards* are achieved brings up the subject of reward and punishment. Here, there are some special how-to's where developing leader skills are *different* from developing individual soldier skills. The differences are extremely important.

Whenever you can, reward the leader *in front of his troops.* And, if you can, reward him more on the basis of what his troops did than what he did personally. Why is this special technique important? It's obviously important for what it does for the individual leader, but it's far *more important* for what it does for the chain of command and for the troops. It strengthens the chain of command by saying, "This link is strong." This builds respect for authority. It works for the troops by saying, "Your leader is good." This builds in the troops that primary thing they need for the battlefield—their confidence.

Reward and punishment apply to training leaders just the same as training any man. Therefore, there are times when leaders must be punished. But, *never* punish or cut down a leader in front of his troops. You can "hurt" him more this way, certainly, but whenever you do it this way, what you're *really* hurting is the chain of command and the troops—their respect for authority and their confidence in the leadership. The chain of command and the troops are far more important than you and your "student."

RELIEVING A LEADER

In extreme cases, punishment of a leader will involve *relieving* that leader. When do you do that? How? Very seldom, and very carefully, primarily because of its impact on respect for authority and confidence in leadership. If you relieve a leader because he fails to meet your own personal standards, watch out. You may not "like" him as a person, but his skill and will may have earned the confidence and respect of his troops. On the other hand, if you relieve a leader who meets neither your standards nor theirs, you *build* confidence in leadership and respect for the chain of command. Some guidelines for this tricky how-to: Relieve *any* leader who lies on significant matters. Relieve a leader who is consistently "unable and unwilling." Relieve a leader whose performance over time begins to lower the SKILL, WILL, and TEAMWORK of his men. Relieve a leader whose errors have serious negative impact on the combat readiness of the unit. Always, in all cases, do it very carefully.

LEADERSHIP MALFUNCTIONS

In the whole process of developing leaders over time, there are two general malfunctions that *will* occur. The leadership of the unit will continue to operate, even with these malfunctions, but it won't run smoothly on all cylinders. One of these malfunctions has to do with **"balancing."**

Two great factors underlie all we know about Army leadership: accomplishment of the mission, and welfare of the men. Mission and men. Leaders are always working with these two basic factors. Whenever and wherever possible, a leader tries to *balance* so that the needs of the mission and the needs of the men are both met. But there are times, sometimes in peace and often in war, when the needs of both cannot be met. You cannot balance. You have to choose one over the other. In these few situations, and you must make them few, **MISSION MUST COME FIRST.** These are those few times when our Army will not, cannot, and should not be "fair." The whole meaning of Army leadership rests on this law of MISSION MUST COME FIRST. So does the meaning of "soldier," and "service," and "duty." You saw that on the very first page, when McFerren went to give his life. Mission came first.

In the balancing business, the "mission" side of the scale requires, simply stated, knowing your job—weapons, gunnery, tactics, mainte-nance—in excruciating detail and with technical competence. Without it, an Army leader can never lead for long. Just talk by itself won't work. Troops know.

The "men" side of the scale requires, simply stated, knowing your soldiers: knowing what's *inside* of them, what makes them do things or not do things; what turns them on, or off; what they can do and what they will do under stress, or when they're afraid or tired or cold or lonely. These are the things you need to know about your soldiers. They're what tells you how a soldier measures up on that "able and willing" gauge.

It is precisely here, in the attempt to balance between these two requirements—mission needs and men needs—that leaders most fre-quently fail. It is here where young sergeants and young lieutenants have their greatest difficulties, and where even old leaders, despite their wis-dom, sometimes lose sight of the ultimate purpose of leadership. The problem arises because of the relationship that exists between soldiers' "happiness and satisfaction," on the one hand, and their "productivity and mission accomplishment," on the other. We have mentioned this point before.

Common sense would tell you that happy, satisfied soldiers will get the job done better. From this, a leader, especially if he's a new sergeant or new lieutenant, might well assume that if he can somehow keep his soldiers happy and satisfied, then they will be more productive, more likely to get the mission accomplished. But the strange chemistry of "leadership" just doesn't work this way. A thousand scientific studies of leadership and a thousand lessons of leadership experience both prove that this natural, commonsense assumption is precisely *wrong!*

Mission accomplishment builds morale and esprit far more often than the other way around. When soldiers and units get done those things that soldiers and units are supposed to do, *that's* when morale and esprit get highest. Just as developing skill affects will, so does mission accomplish-ment build morale. That's why unit esprit is at its peak when the unit has a good FTX going out in the field. Mission accomplishment drives morale far more often than the other way around.

If leaders don't know both sides of the "leadership scale"—the needs of the *mission* and the needs of the *men*—in full detail, they'll be forever getting the scale tilted the wrong way. And when that happens, the soldiers' time or the soldiers' spirit or the soldiers themselves will be wasted.

Twice before in this book, we've discussed the matter of *mission and men.* In the final analysis, when the artillery shifts there on the battlefield for which you are now preparing, **MISSION MUST COME FIRST.** As you build leaders, this "law" has to be, flat-out, the cornerstone of your foundation.

The second general leadership malfunction that will occur in the process of developing leaders will do so when the leadership of the unit puts insufficient effort into recognizing, emphasizing, and using THE DIFFERENCE.

Of the 169 men in a full strength company, 43 are *officers* and 126 are *not*. Forty-three are in *the leadership of the unit* and 126 are *not*. And that's THE DIFFERENCE. There is a "line" between those who are the leaders and those who are not. The line is totally *unimportant* in terms of making the 43 "better" than the 126. Any one of the 169 can be as good a soldier as any other. The line is *extremely important,* however, in terms of making it possible for the leadership of the unit to lead. Any organized effort involving two or more people must have someone in charge. There must be leaders and followers. Leaders and followers do different things. Leaders analyze, organize, deputize, and supervise. Followers execute. The line establishes THE DIFFERENCE between the two.

We previously discussed the differences between commissioned officers and noncommissioned officers (Chapter 3). Then, when we tackled that list of 100 things on the desks in the Orderly Room, you saw how using the officer–NCO difference made it much easier to get those 100 tasks *done*. What makes this work is knowing THE DIFFERENCE. The same principle applies to knowing THE DIFFERENCE between leaders and followers in the whole unit. New Lieutenants and new sergeants, just as they have a hard time "balancing" between mission needs and men needs, also have a hard time learning THE DIFFERENCE between leaders and followers.

Go back to that young "able and willing" soldier down in the Motor Pool, the one you started on the road to becoming a leader. You picked him out because he seemed to be the "main man" in one of those informal buddy groups. Now why do you think his buddies looked at him as the main man? It was because he knew better than anyone else what was *inside* his buddies: how they felt about the Army and about their job; what their attitude was; what their needs were. And he was "main man" also because he, better than anyone else, could act as their spokesman in passing on their attitudes and needs to the leadership. That's what makes an informal leader of a good group *or* a sorry group. He knows his buddies' attitudes and needs, and they think he's the one who can most probably get something done about them. That's why they put him "in charge," informally. Then you put him "in charge," formally. You did right, because he's a leader, in your eyes and theirs.

This young man, as an informal leader, is expert in "needs of the men." But at this stage, there is no way he can do the balancing which we said earlier was so critical. He knows little about "needs of the mission." When you bring him across that line that separates leaders from followers, "needs of the mission" are what he must learn. Then, when he's started learning that, he will begin to understand the price he has to pay to become a leader of men. Nothing good ever comes free. What he will learn is that never again, as a leader, can he be "one of the boys." He's across the line. Graduated. Different.

Since he's different now, he's got to find some new "buddy groups." He's got to "hang around" with leaders, and not with "the boys." And that's why brand-new sergeants should be reassigned within the unit; and that's why, in good units, there are separate areas in the Mess Hall where sergeants can talk about "sergeants' business"; and that's why, in good units, there are separate NCO clubs where they can talk about it some more; and why there are separate NCO rooms in the barracks; and why there are separate NCO functions and activities. All this has nothing to do with "NCO prestige." The purpose of all this separating is to teach, to develop, to strengthen, to make clear, THE DIFFERENCE between those who are part of the leadership and those who are not. The better *the leadership* of the unit does this separating, the better *the unit* is led.

So much for two general malfunctions that are bound to occur in the process of developing leaders.

SOLDIER VALUES

In laying out the how-to's for developing leaders, we're going to cover one last subject. It is the most important subject in this book and in this whole Army. It is MOST IMPORTANT, but it is also LEAST SPECIFIC. No step-by-step how-to's. The subject is soldier values. Values build *discipline.* You'll see why in a moment.

Go find a handful of unit crests. Read the words. What those mottoes say is what those different units want to be, what they aspire to be, how they want to be known, what they want to be known for, what they want their reputation to be based on, and what people can expect of them. Those words tell you "what's important" in those units. Values are nothing more than a few words that describe "what's important."

If you think back to one of the really fine units you've been in, you'll most probably find that you can recall the words of the unit's motto. If you think a little more, you'll remember that there were times when those words gave you some guidance about what you, as a member of the outfit should do. The words helped you make decisions. Helped you figure out what was "right." Values guide leaders to do the *right* things.

Any unit or organization must have values—those few words that say "what's important" for that outfit and lead leaders to make the right decisions and do the right things. Now if you'll think about the words on all those unit crests, you'll see that those words usually talk about what is "most important" in terms of that unit accomplishing its mission: its purpose.

Our Army's purpose, as we've said before, is to fight and win the land battle. That means our Army's purpose gets accomplished . . . on the battlefield. And that means that a soldier's values must serve some function *when the unit fights.* Many experienced small-unit combat leaders feel there are about four soldier values that do this. Four words. They come from all the words on all those unit crests put together. They represent what we want our soldiers to be. They describe what our nation expects of its soldiers. Finally, and most important, they serve our Army's purpose on the battlefield, *when the unit fights.* The four words are CANDOR, COMMITMENT, COURAGE, and COMPETENCE. Each one affects the other.

CANDOR. This is not a very "strong" word, but here in this book, it means openness *plus* honesty *plus* simplicity. On the battlefield, it is the prime rule governing communications among men. It operates to ensure the best possible transfer of *meaning* among people. The stakes are too high, and time is too short, to screw around with anything else but the essence and the truth. Men in battle can't mess around with little white lies and private secrets and little games. Communication of fact, and of feelings as well, must be clean, simple, whole, accurate.

The candor of the battlefield serves to develop and support the trust upon which men's commitment to each other is built. The candor of the battlefield is why "buddy groups" form there so quickly and permanently. The candor of the battlefield is why lies told there are punished, not with gossip, but with action.

The battlefield is the most honest place in the world.

COMMITMENT. Battlefield commitment is mainly to men and groups of men, far more than to things. For the soldier, it is commitment first to that ole buddy, then close after that, commitment to the squad or the crew. Some commitment to larger units and a little to the nation, but not near as much as to the buddy and the squad. This value operates to provide security, which comes from mutual trust. It also serves as the central foundation for teamwork and coordination. Basic training gets this value started.

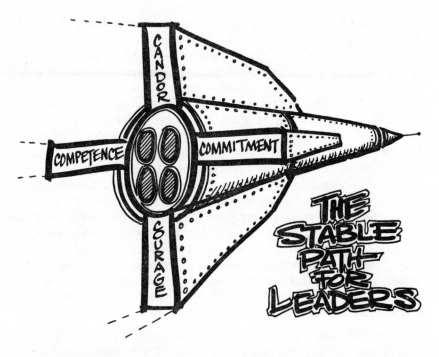

Fire and maneuver and combined arms teamwork, the underpinnings of the whole way we fight, are a function of the strength of commitment to men and groups of men—commitment to each other, to the "US" in U.S. Army.

Leaders' commitment to men focuses downward, to the troops. The strength of this downward commitment often decreases as leader rank increases. In a way, what happens as rank increases is that commitment to men begins to change into commitment to purpose or mission.

Commitment to other soldiers is the main message in most Congressional Medal of Honor citations.

COURAGE. Courage is taking a risk even though the choice not to do so is open. On the battlefield, the risk is a total-loss risk, and yet, for various reasons the soldier *himself* decides that the total-loss risk is his best choice. This risk taking is the ultimate definition of "soldier." That's why some people say that to be a soldier is "the noblest act of mankind."

Courage in individuals turns the whole action on. The action cannot start without courage on the part of an individual. That's what battle leaders do, and what the green tab is supposed to mean, and why SET THE EXAMPLE is always so important. Further, the action cannot continue to its conclusion unless courage continues, not just by the leader, but by all involved. In battle, in the unit, courage grows from an individual trait into a process.

There is a contagion to courage, and it spreads most rapidly in cohesive units.

COMPETENCE. The oldest value on the battlefield. Ten thousand years ago, 'way back even before there were such things as "armies," 'way back when it was one-on-one, competence determined who won.

Competence is also the central value, since the other three are linked to it. On the battlefield, candor is important only to ensure accurate transfer of meaning about the changing status of competence. Competence is the basis for skill and for confidence in one's self, which is where courage comes from. Competence is also the basis for confidence in others, which establishes commitment, since the patterns and strength of trust and mutual support are formed on the basis of where competence lies and in what degree.

On the battlefield, it is competence that establishes status and "pecking order," and so the patterns of strong informal leadership which actually "run" the action may or may not correspond to the formal pattern or actual chain of command. This depends on the competence of the formal "chain" and each of its members.

On the battlefield subordinates, buddies, and superiors value competence more than any other attribute — except courage.

That's what those four soldier values do on the battlefield. How can you use them in developing leaders? Well, think a moment about the "Traits of a Leader." Those four words summarize the traits. Think about the "Principles of Leadership." Those four words summarize the principles. Since this is so, and since you're a leader, and since you know that the one best way to lead is to SET THE EXAMPLE, then develop your subordinate leaders in the best possible way: *you* show them, every day, what those values look like when a leader leads.

If they do the same, then *every* soldier in the unit begins to understand "what's important." The more that occurs, the greater the chance that every soldier will do the *right* thing on his own. And isn't that what "discipline" means?

5

Small-Unit Teamwork

THE BASIC MECHANICS OF TEAMWORK

A hundred thousand years ago, when "war" was first invented, soldiering was pretty simple. "Armies" were small: about ten men. There was one officer: the biggest and meanest. There was one uniform: a piece of animal skin. There was one weapon: a club. And one MOS: 11B. And one tactic: hand-to-hand, man-to-man. If the numbers were about equal, what won on that battlefield then was SKILL and WILL.

Ten thousand years later on the battlefield, things had changed. Those small armies were bigger: a hundred men now, organized into ten groups of ten men each. There was a chain of command, and eleven officers: one leader for each group of ten, plus one biggest and meanest leader of the leaders. There were two more uniform items: footgear, and shields. And two new kinds of weapons: bows and arrows, and long spears carried by men on horses. And two new MOS's: 13E and 19B. Tactics were more complicated. The infantrymen still did just about what they had done before, but the cavalrymen, with their long spears and horses, had to coordinate their faster speed with the movement of the slower infantrymen. And the artillerymen had to learn to shoot their arrows *before* their infantry and cavalry buddies got going with their clubs and spears in the hand-to-hand business. With that, the two basics of *all* combat teamwork were born: fire, and maneuver.

What won on this newer battlefield was SKILL and WILL and **TEAM-**

WORK. And it was discovered on countless battlefields after that that an army of a hundred men who could work together as a combined arms *team* could whip the daylights out of an army of a thousand men who couldn't.

Ever since that time, as war and weapons have become more complex, TEAMWORK has become more and more the deciding factor on the battlefield. Military history points this out time and time again. That's why we have stressed the importance of you, as a leader, working to build SKILL, WILL, and **TEAMWORK.** That's why the tenth principle of leadership, which carries with it the wisdom of war, holds you responsible to TRAIN YOUR MEN AS A TEAM.

In this chapter on building teamwork, we're going to develop the tenth principle in detail. The complexity of the battlefield for which you are preparing, coupled with the fact that you must fight and win outnumbered, make TEAMWORK more important for Army leadership today than it has ever been. It is in teamwork that we can find that "extra" that wins.

Suppose that, through some military magic and a mighty individual training effort, the leadership of your unit had been able to develop to standards every single one of the fifteen hundred *individual* skills that the unit needs. What would you have? You'd have 169 individuals you could be proud of, but that's about all. If individual skills were the only kind of skills you had, then the company, the unit, would not survive on the battlefield. Individual skills must be *put together.*

The business of *putting things together* is basically what teamwork is. *Putting together* is the responsibility of the leadership of the unit. Fire-team leaders put together the individual skills of soldiers and build a *team.* Squad leaders put together two fire teams and build a larger *team* called a squad. Platoon leaders put together four squads and build a larger *team* called a platoon. And the company commander puts platoons together to build the basic fighting *team* of the U.S. Army. That deadly "thing" on the battlefield that we discussed several chapters back is a combat *team.* All the parts, put together, functioning smoothly, as a *whole.* As a *team.* In the deadly business of delivering steel.

There are three different kinds of teamwork. What makes the difference is (1) how much the individuals in the team have to *depend* on each other, and (2) how much the leader must *control* the actions of the individuals.

The simplest kind of teamwork is like a bowling team. Each individual by himself does the best he can, then individual scores are added up to determine how well the "team" did. There's not much real teamwork involved. Individuals are not dependent on each other, and the leader has little to do in the way of coordinating and controlling their actions. His main task in this case is to train and motivate *individuals.* When a unit is firing on the rifle range, it is functioning basically as this kind of a team.

Things get a little more complicated with a relay team in a track meet. Individual skill (speed) is critical, but now in this kind of teamwork, each team member must do his task right *before* the next man can start to do his. Leaders still work to fire up individual performance, but now they concentrate on the part of the action and the point in time when the individuals depend on each other—the handoff. And if even one runner, even the "World's Fastest Human," drops the stick, the *team* loses. There are many examples of this kind of teamwork in a military unit. The mechanic down in the Motor Pool must get the CO's vehicle running *before* the CO can get to the field to coordinate and control the FTX.

The third and most complex kind of teamwork is the kind you find in a football team. Every individual is dependent on everyone else. If one man, like the center, or one "fire team," like the linemen, fail to do the right things right, that can cause the team as a whole to lose. The leader of this most complex kind of team is concerned about motivation, but more importantly, he is most concerned about how to coordinate and control the actions of every single individual. To win, the team as a whole must "get it all together." War is not a game, but the best military example of this most complex kind of teamwork occurs on the battlefield. There, the leadership of the unit puts that whole "thing" together, and it *fights.*

You have seen, in these three examples, a principle that we have emphasized before: "Different strokes for different folks." This means that you, as a leader, must do different things according to the kind of teamwork involved. If the requirement is for excellence of individual performance, then build and control the team by carefully explaining and closely supervising the individual training and individual motivation. If the teamwork requirement is for a sequence of actions to be performed by different individuals one after the other, then build and control the team by concentrating on the times and places where one man "hands off" to the next. Finally, if the teamwork requirement is the one in which everyone is dependent on everyone else—and this is *the battlefield kind* of teamwork—then there is only one way to build and control the team. You already know what it is, don't you?

Your requirement as a leader in this most complicated of the three kinds of teamwork is to control each action of each man so that all the pieces of the action fit together right. To do this, you must control *what* each man does, *how* he does it, and *when* he does it. If you're a squad leader or higher, you've got to be controlling, not subordinate individual soldiers, but your subordinate *teams. What* they do, *how* they do it, *when* they do it. And you do this through the chain—through your subordinate leaders. Clear, uncomplicated orders and clear, uncomplicated communications will help, but even with these, there is *no way* you can watch over and control, constantly, what every man and team does or how they do it or when they do it.

The only way you can build the kind of control essential for battlefield teamwork is to build that control into the individuals and teams themselves. Build *internal* control. And there's only one way to do that, the same way the football coach does: DRILL. Practice and critique, practice and critique, practice and critique. Over and over, until individuals and teams *learn* to control themselves; until they *learn* where, when, and how they are dependent on one another; until the individuals and teams *learn* what each individual and each team must do in order to "get it all together." DRILL.

Football coaches call these drills "scrimmages," and they write them down in playbooks. Army leaders call these drills "collective tasks" or "battle drills," and they write them down in ARTEP manuals. Coaches that win on the playing field and leaders that win on the battlefield will both tell you the same thing: you must start with good basic individual skills as a foundation. Coaches say, "Run, block, and tackle." Battle leaders say, "Move, shoot, and communicate." After that, it's DRILL and DRILL and DRILL. DRILL until *working together* becomes instinct. And DRILL toward perfection. Practice *doesn't* make perfect. What makes perfect is perfect practice. DRILL.

Basic individual SKILL, the WILL to work to get ready, and TEAMWORK drill. That's the only road that leads to winning teams. Now we can lay out another simple, basic "formula" of leadership arithmetic:

SKILL × WILL × DRILL = KILL

At this point, you know the three basic kinds of teamwork. You know also that each different kind requires you to lead in a different way. You know that the toughest kind of teamwork is the kind required on the battlefield, where men and teams are all *interdependent* on each other; and you know that the one best solution for building that kind of teamwork is DRILL. You've got a handle on what teamwork *is,* and you have a general idea of how to build it. We will get to some of the specific how-to's for building teamwork in a moment, but right now, it's time to look at some military examples and see what teamwork *does* and how teamwork *works.*

TEAMWORK: THE INDIVIDUAL FIGHTING POSITION

Find a copy of the current manual on squad and platoon tactics and look up one of the most fundamental things on the battlefield—The Individual Fighting Position. Study the diagrams, and you'll see how teamwork *works.* PFCs first invented and developed this new fighting position in our last war. After that war, colonels directed tests and analyses of the effectiveness of the position, and after that, generals made it part of our Army's standard "how-to-fight" doctrine.

The new position is far more effective than the fighting position we used before. Effective in terms of *more* enemy and *fewer* friendly killed. But one of these new positions, by itself, won't get this kind of effectiveness. It takes at least two positions, *put together.* Look at the diagram. When these positions are put together *right,* they are about three times more effective than the position we used in earlier wars. This "three times more effective" is one of those "extras" that we have discussed many times before. You get it when you get things *put together* in just the right way. It is an extra that pays off in enemy killed on the battlefield, an extra that occurs when soldiers in these new fighting positions work *together* as a team, with men in one fighting position *dependent upon* men in another.

Study the diagram some more. You'll see that the men in one position have to *trust* the men in the other. This is a basic part of teamwork. Members of battlefield teams have to learn to trust one another. That's not easy to do when lives are at stake. How do men learn whether to trust

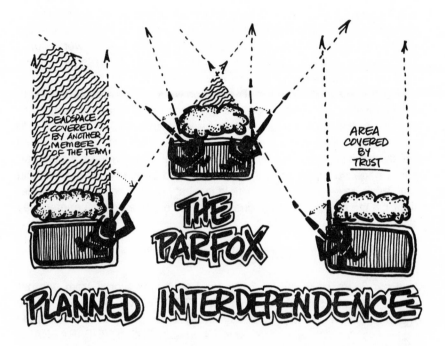

one another? This is one of the many things that DRILL does. Builds trust. DRILL gives men the opportunity to *see* how competent the other people on whom they have to depend are. Many times, if a man doesn't *know,* or doesn't *want,* to do his job right, then the men who are dependent upon him will see to it that he *learns* and *wants.* Repeated DRILL brings increased competence, and increased competence leads to increased trust. So, when PFC Jones in that new individual fighting position *trusts* PFC Smith in the adjacent position to keep his front covered, then PFC Jones can concentrate even more on killing enemy and worry less about getting killed himself. A quarterback who *trusts* his linemen to keep him from getting "sacked" can hit his receivers with far greater accuracy. Drill builds competence. Competence builds trust. Trust builds teamwork. And teamwork gets the "extra."

TEAMWORK: DISMOUNTED DRILL

You can learn another lesson about how teamwork works by thinking about dismounted drill. Two hundred years ago, the purpose of dismounted drill was to teach soldiers the kind of close-packed formations and movements actually used on those old battlefields. Why do we still use those formations today? Why do we still spend so much time teaching dismounted drill in Basic Training, and, later on, teaching dismounted drill to men and units who already know how to drill? The answer is *not* to teach "instantaneous obedience to orders," although that's partly true. And the answer is *not* to control and move units in an orderly fashion, although that's partly true too. The reason we teach dismounted drill is to teach the soldier that he is part of a *team,* and that that *team* is something bigger and far more important than he is as an individual. He learns to work as a part of a *whole* thing. He learns to adjust what he does to what others are doing. And he also learns that one little screw-up on his part has a negative effect on the whole unit, and on every member of that unit. What he *learns* on the drill field is what he must *know* on the battlefield. On the battlefield, when one man gets "out of step," other men may die.

TEAMWORK: FIVE-PARAGRAPH FIELD ORDER

You can learn some more about how teamwork works from another basic: THE FIVE-PARAGRAPH FIELD ORDER. You should memorize this basic, then use it in your day-to-day order-giving until it becomes instinctive. You should memorize it because THE FIVE-PARAGRAPH FIELD ORDER is a clear, concise, and complete format for communicating "What to do," and it covers all the required essentials. But it also does something else. Something even more important. If you'll think about the format of THE FIVE-PARAGRAPH FIELD ORDER, you'll see that it's *designed* to set the stage for effective teamwork.

Situation describes the big picture of what's going on, enemy and friendly. If all members of the team have this same big picture, then each member can better understand the "why" for what it is the team's going to be told to do. They can see how their team fits together with other teams and larger teams. A *shared* "big picture" gets all members of the team up on the same frequency.

Mission lays out, specifically, what the team as a whole is going to get accomplished. There is no way that the *parts* of a team can work effectively unless they know what it is that the *whole* team is trying to get done. Mission gives all team members the same "sense of purpose."

Concept of Operation is the plan for the team as a whole. It lays out *how* the parts of the team must work together to get the task accomplished. A plan of maneuver and a plan of fire support are always part of the concept. In the Concept of Operation, these two basics of combat teamwork are *coordinated,* just as they were thousands of years ago when teamwork on the battlefield was first invented.

Subparagraphs that follow the Concept of Operation lay out a specific subtask for each part of the whole team. When each part can hear, see, and know what each other part is supposed to do, then each of the parts has a better chance to adjust and time its own actions to what the other parts are doing, once the action starts. The Subparagraphs help all the parts to *work together.*

Coordinating Instructions identify the most critical times and places where two or more parts are dependent on each other. These times and places are like the "handoffs" we discussed earlier. They are the times and places where coordination is so critical that the parts can't be given the leeway to adjust to each other.

Command and Signal lays out who it is that the parts of the team will take directions from, and how and where they will get this information. This section of THE FIVE-PARAGRAPH FIELD ORDER ensures that all parts of the team get their guidance and orders from the *same* place, namely, the chain of command—always the center of coordination and control when the action gets started and each part starts doing its part.

From this discussion, it should be easy to see that if a leader at any level makes maximum use of THE FIVE-PARAGRAPH FIELD ORDER all the time, then he is, at the same time, teaching his team how teamwork works—"Training his men as a team." And this is a far better way to do it than by giving a class or a speech about "teamwork."

TEAMWORK: STRATEGY AND TECHNIQUES

In the preceding sections, you have seen what teamwork *is.* We have also discussed three military examples of teamwork so that you can get the general idea of how teamwork *works.* Study the examples and you'll see that each one also gives you some guidance for how to *build* a team. We will now lay out for you an overall team-building strategy, then follow that with about a dozen more ways to "train your men as a team."

Fire-team leaders build teams out of subordinate individual soldiers. Squad leaders and above build teams out of subordinate leaders and *their* teams. In either case, there is one simple overall leadership strategy for building a team. This is a *strategy*—an overall way of operating—not a specific how-to. The strategy has two requirements for you.

You, as the leader, must constantly, on a day-to-day basis, do things and say things that will convince each individual team member that he is a part of a *whole* team. And not just a plain ol' part, but an essential part— a part that other team members depend upon to get *their* work done, and that the whole team depends upon to get *its* work done.

The second requirement of the strategy is that you do and say things on a day-to-day basis to convince the individual team member that *his* wants, needs, hopes, goals, and so on are tied to the performance, output, and work of the *team.* Each individual team member, just like you, will normally operate in his own best interest. He'll do what he thinks is best for *him.* That's a fact of human nature. In building a team, you have to work to convince each team member that the best way for him to get what *he* wants is through what the *team* does.

In summary, this team-building leadership "strategy" says: (1) convince each team member that other team members and the team as a whole are *dependent* on him and (2) convince him that much of the whole business of reward and punishment, for *him,* is tied to the output or performance of the *team.* Doing all this convincing is not easy. At first you're going to have to spend some time figuring out *how* to do it. Keep at it, and it will become automatic.

Building the complex kind of team that the battlefield requires is tough. Takes time. Takes thinking ahead. Takes knowing the sixth principle of leadership—KNOW YOUR SOLDIERS and know what's *inside* each man. Beyond the general strategy, there is no step-by-step formula that is very practical for use by company-level leaders. There are, however, about a dozen good team-building techniques which come from experience and research, and which will *work* for captains, lieutenants, and sergeants.

● The *best* way to build the kind of team the unit needs is the way we've already explained—DRILL. The best DRILLS for this are spelled out in the ARTEPs. If you can't get out in the field, do it on the parade ground. If you can't do that, try a blackboard or a terrain model or a map. *Always* critique a DRILL. Critique the performance of the *team* and how each individual team member contributed, or failed to contribute, to the *team's* performance.

● High stress and heavy pressure applied to the whole team will build teamwork. Events, exercises, and activities that are extreme challenges and that demand a hard-core, all-out effort by the team and each team member *will* build teamwork. Add danger, and teamwork gets even stronger. The high stress of battle puts teams together so well that they continue to have annual "get-togethers" for years after the war is over. In training, get as close to battlefield stress as you can. Without a war, Captain, try a hundred-mile road march; or run ten with weapons, helmets, and LBE; or climb a mountain; or run a super-tough, nonstop, day-and-night, twenty-four-hour battle drill over the worst terrain you can find. Do any or all of these high-stress events as a *team.* It'll work.

● Get tasks done by *teams,* rather than "details." First Sergeant, you can do a lot about this. Next time battalion hits you up for "a ten-man detail and one NCO," check into the chain first, but then send, not just a "detail," but a fire team with its own team leader. Chances are good that half as many men, working as a *team,* can do twice as much work. Bet on it, and let the team know you bet.

• Whenever there are formations, leave *teams* together. "Break off and fill it up back there!" may make the platoon formation *look* better, Lieutenant, but what you're breaking up is teamwork. How units *work* is about a hundred times more important than how they look. And as a commissioned officer, you're supposed to be a leadership specialist in *unit* work.

• Whenever you, Sergeant, as the leader, must form your men, brief your men, move your men, work your men, critique your men, feed your men, or billet your men, then do it the same way you're going to have to *fight* your men on the battlefield—as a team. You can tell your troops, "Everyone be down at the Motor Pool at 1300 to clean the tracks." That's the way a Boy Scout leader might do it. It may (or may not) get them all there by somewhere around 1330. And, Sergeant, you've just lost one of those valuable day-to-day opportunities to keep working on teamwork. Form them up as a squad in the company area, march them to the Motor Pool, in step, stand them at ease, give them their instructions with something like THE FIVE-PARAGRAPH FIELD ORDER (including *standards* in the mission part), supervise the fire-team leaders, keep the *whole* squad at it until the *whole* job is done, form them up again, critique their performance as a *team,* march the whole squad back to the company area, and only *then* turn them loose to be individuals. Keep this up, time after time, day after day, until it becomes the "natural" way the squad does things. If you, as the leader, can keep your subordinates working and living as a *team* in their day-to-day activities, those ARTEP drills will come out far better, and so will that "thing" on the battlefield.

• Up on the wall in the Orderly Room or the CO's office, there's a "manning board." It is a main tool for building and maintaining teamwork. The First Sergeant and the platoon leaders will be making the primary recommendations about who goes where, but the CO will be making the decisions. *Never* move a name around, Captain, without first thinking about the impact on teamwork. When you move names around in an attempt to "even out" strength figures, you may be doing the same thing as when the lieutenant "evens up" the platoon formation. The board may *look* better, but your unit may *work* worse because you've unintentionally destroyed some of your teamwork power. Some of that "extra."

Each time you move a name, what you're really moving is a *man,* and you're moving him out of his "family." Put that under "Welfare of the

Troops." More importantly, when you move him, you're moving a *part* of something bigger. If that "something bigger" is a smoothly functioning team—a "fighting machine"—then you may be pulling out the carburetor. And a carburetor can't be replaced with an oil pump. You can put that under "Mission." As a general rule, hold manning board moves to an absolute bare minimum, and *always* consider first the impact on the team of which the soldier is a part.

● There is a simple, guaranteed way that *all* leaders can build teamwork. Simply start using the *team* words—"WE," "OUR," and "US" instead of the three *individual* words, "I," "Me," and "My." When a leader starts leading by example with his language, followers will follow. And they'll start talking and thinking more about "US" than about "Me." The *first* two letters in U.S. Army are "US." The *last* two are "My." Think about that.

● Any man will work hard to live up to his *reputation.* So will a team. Whenever a team does something that is both unusual and good, and they do it as a team, let all the leadership of the whole unit know about it. When this happens three or four times, the word will get back to the team. At that point, they'll find out that *they* have a reputation to live up to.

● Whenever you're supervising a task that requires a high degree of teamwork (as with the football team example we discussed), then try to gear your supervision, critique, reward, and punishment to what the *team* does more than to what *individuals* do. Do it in such a way that each individual can see that what *he* wants most (or wants least) depends more on what the *team* does than on what *he* does. Punishing a whole team is extremely effective, but do it very carefully. You wouldn't punish a whole relay team just because "World's Fastest Human" got careless and dropped the stick. Punish a whole team when *all* the handoffs are too sloppy or too slow; when there's no trust among the parts; or when all the parts get to thinking more about "Me" than about "US."

● Next to DRILL, the best thing for building teamwork is that all-powerful, all-purpose leadership tool we've mentioned so many times before—the fifth principle of leadership, SET THE EXAMPLE. If you're a squad leader, do you want your followers to believe that, for them, the *squad's* mission is the most important thing there is? If so, then show them that for you, the *platoon's* mission is the most important thing there is. If you're a squad leader, *never* complain about the platoon's mission or the platoon leader in front of your followers. If you do, they're going to follow your example and do the same about *your* mission and *you.* Do you want your followers to cooperate, work together, and trust each other? Then show them, by example, that that's exactly how *you* work with other squad leaders. From the Motor Pool to the battlefield, in *any* situation, followers will do as their *leaders* do. Good or bad.

• What makes your team *different* from other teams? Find out what those differences are and keep emphasizing them to your teams. It may be the kind of work they do or where they do it or when they do it. Whatever makes them different from other teams. This is another way of telling team members that *their* team is something special, something different, something important. Want to build some teamwork in your company, Captain? Well, one thing that's *always* different in any unit is the unit's history. Send a letter up through channels and find out what A Company did in the last war or two. Then sit down sometime and tell the troops about *their* team at war and how it fought in wars in the past. Do this two or three times, covering two or three wars, and watch what happens with "teamwork." Sergeant, you can do the same thing with a shorter view of history. What are the four or five best things the squad has done as a *team* in the last year or six months? Remind the squad about these from time to time.

In the paragraphs above, we've discussed about a dozen specific techniques of how to build teamwork. In the three military examples before that, we covered maybe six more specific techniques. Back at the first of the chapter, where we explained the three *kinds* of teamwork, we spelled out two or three more techniques for building teamwork according to the kind of teamwork involved. That's twenty-four how-to's for teamwork. And somewhere back in there, we laid out a two-part team-building *strategy* for you to keep working on *all* the time—no matter what technique or tactics you might be using. Now it's time to look at teamwork . . . on the battlefield.

TEAMWORK: ON THE BATTLEFIELD

Ten thousand miles away, in Vietnam, there is a hilltop that rises up out of the jungle just to the west of the town of Chulai. Today, it is overgrown and quiet—just another insignificant hilltop, known more by its number than by its name.

It wasn't always that way. There was once a time when for a period of several days that hilltop, blasted by airstrikes and artillery into a jumble of raw earth and rocks, trembled and shook with the thunder and fire of battle. At that time, that hill belonged to a guy named Howard. And in the minds of many men today, it is still known as "Howard's Hill."

Howard was a small-unit leader—an NCO. His full name was Jimmie Earl Howard. He was a staff sergeant. As NCOs often are in combat, he was also an acting platoon leader. He had only seventeen men in his platoon. There on Howard's Hill, that seventeen-man platoon took on, fought with, and beat the daylights out of, a full-strength, well-equipped, highly trained North Vietnamese Regular Army *battalion.*

Staff Sergeant Howard's platoon "fought outnumbered," and they won. They did it with TEAMWORK—teamwork among the men in the platoon, among the teams within the platoon, among the combat support and combat service units that came to help them, and among the other Army and Air Force elements that also became part of Staff Sergeant Howard's team there on Howard's Hill.

As you read this battle story, selected from our sister service because it is such a clear example of combat teamwork at the small-unit level, think about the mechanics of teamwork and all we have discussed so far about how it is developed. Watch teamwork at work—on the battlefield.

Some twenty miles inland to the west of Chulai runs a range of steep mountains and twisting valleys. In that bandits' lair, the Viet Cong and North Vietnamese could train and plan for attacks against the heavily populated seacoast hamlets, massing only when it was time to attack. In early June of 1966, the intelligence reports reaching III MAF headquarters indicated that a mixed force of Viet Cong and North Vietnamese was gathering by the thousands in those mountains. But the enemy leaders were not packing their troops into a few large, vulnerable assembly points; they kept their units widely dispersed, moving mainly in squads and platoons.

To frustrate that scheme and keep the enemy off balance, the Marines launched Operation KANSAS, an imaginative concept in strategy. Rather than send full infantry battalions to beat the bushes in search of small enemy bands, Lieutenant General Lewis W. Walt detailed the reconnaissance battalion of the 1st Marine Division to scout the mountains. The reconnaissance Marines would move in small teams of eight to twenty men. If they located a large enemy concentration, Marine infantry would be flown in. If, as was expected, they saw only numerous small groups of Viet Cong and North Vietnamese, they were to smash them by calling in air and artillery strikes.

Lieutenant Colonel Arthur J. Sullivan had set high training standards for his battalion. Every man had received individual schooling in forward observer techniques and reconnaissance patrol procedures. He was confident his men could perform the mission successfully, despite the obvious hazards. "The Vietnam war," he said, "has given the small-unit leader— the corporal, the sergeant, the lieutenant—a chance to be independent. The senior officers just can't be out there looking over their shoulders. You have to have confidence in your junior officers and NCOs."

One such NCO was Staff Sergeant Jimmie Earl Howard, acting commander of the 1st Platoon, Charlie Company, 1st Reconnaissance Battalion. A tall, well-built man in his mid-thirties, leadership came naturally to him. "Howard was a very personable fellow," his company commander, Captain Tim Geraghty, said. "The men liked him. They liked to work for him."

As dusk fell on the evening of 13 June 1966, a flight of helicopters settled on the slope of Hill 488, twenty-five miles west of Chulai. Howard and his seventeen men jumped out and climbed the steep incline to the top. The hill, called Nui Vu, rose to a peak of nearly fifteen hundred feet and dominated the terrain for miles. Three narrow strips of level ground ran along the top for several hundred yards before falling abruptly away. Seen from the air, they roughly resembled the three blades on an airplane propeller. Howard chose the blade which pointed north for his command post and placed observation teams on the other two blades. It was an ideal vantage point.

The enemy knew the hill also. Their foxholes dotted the ground, each with a small shelter scooped out two feet under the surface. Howard permitted his men use of these one-man caves during the day to avoid the hot sun and enemy detection. There was no other cover or concealment to be found. There were no trees, only knee-high grass and small scrub growth.

In the surrounding valleys and villages, there were many enemy. For the next two days, Howard was constantly calling for fire missions, as members of the platoon saw small enemy groups almost every hour. Not all the requests for air and artillery strikes were honored. Sullivan was concerned lest the platoon's position, so salient and bare, be spotted by a suspicious enemy. Most of the firing at targets located by the platoon was done only when there was an observation plane circling in the vicinity to decoy the enemy. After two days Sullivan and his executive officer, Major Allan Harris, became alarmed at the risk involved in leaving the platoon stationary any longer. But the observation post was ideal; Howard had encountered no difficulty, and, in any case, thought he had a secure escape route along a ridge to the east. So it was decided to leave the platoon on Nui Vu for one more day.

However, the enemy were well aware of the platoon's presence. (Sullivan had a theory that the Viet Cong and North Vietnamese, long harassed, disrupted, and punished by reconnaissance units in territory they claimed to control absolutely, had determined to eliminate one such unit, hoping thereby to demoralize the others. Looked at in hindsight, the ferocity and tenacity of the attack upon Nui Vu gives credence to the colonel's theory.) In any case, the North Vietnamese made their preparations well and did not tip their hand. On 15 June, they moved a fresh, well-equipped, highly trained battalion to the base of Nui Vu. In late afternoon hundreds of the enemy started to climb up the three blades, hoping to annihilate the dozen and a half Marines in one surprise attack.

The Army Special Forces frustrated that plan. Sergeant 1st Class Donald Reed and Specialist 5th Class Hardey Drande were leading a platoon of CIDG (Civilian Irregular Defense Group) forces on patrol near Nui

Vu that same afternoon. They saw elements of the North Vietnamese battalion moving towards the hill and radioed the news back to their base camp at Hoi An, several miles to the south. Howard's radio was purposely set on the same frequency and so he was alerted at the same time. Reed and Drande wanted to hit the enemy from the rear and disrupt them, but had to abandon the idea when they suddenly found themselves a very unpopular minority of two on the subject. Describing the reactions of the Special Forces NCOs later, Howard could not resist chuckling. "The language those sergeants used over the radio," he said, "when they realized they couldn't attack the NVA, well, they sure didn't learn it at communications school." Even though the Special Forces were not able to provide the ground support they wished to, their warning alerted Howard and enabled him to develop a precise defensive plan before the attack was launched.

Acting on the NCOs' report, Howard gathered his team leaders, briefed them on the situation, selected an assembly point, instructed them to stay on full alert and to withdraw to the main position at the first sign of an approaching enemy. The corporals and lance corporals crept back to their teams and briefed them in the growing dusk. The Marines then settled down to watch and wait.

Lance Corporal Ricardo Binns had placed his observation team on the slope forty meters forward of Howard's position. At approximately 2200, while the four Marines were lying in a shallow depression discussing in whispers their sergeant's solemn warnings, Binns quite casually propped himself up on his elbows and placed his rifle butt in his shoulder. Without saying a word, he pointed the barrel at a bush and fired. The bush pitched backward and fell thrashing twelve feet away.

The other Marines jumped up. Each threw a grenade, before grabbing his rifle and scrambling up the hill. Behind them grenades burst and automatic weapons pounded away. The battle of Nui Vu was on.

The other outposts withdrew to the main position. The Marines commanded a tiny rock-strewn knoll. The rocks would provide some protection for the defenders. Placing his two radios behind a large boulder, Howard set up a tight circular perimeter, not over twenty meters in diameter, and selected a firing position for each Marine.

The North Vietnamese too were setting up. They had made no audible noises while climbing. There was no talking, no clumsy movements. When Binns killed one of their scouts, they were less than fifty meters from the top.

The Marines were surrounded. From all sides the enemy threw grenades. Some bounced off the rocks; some rolled back down the slopes; some did not explode, but some landed right on Marines and did explode. The next day the platoon corpsman, Billie Don Holmes, recalled: "They were within twenty feet of us. Suddenly there were grenades all over. Then people started hollering. It seemed everyone got hit at the same time."

Holmes crawled forward to help. A grenade exploded between him and a wounded man. Holmes lost consciousness.

The battle was going well for the North Vietnamese. Four .50-caliber machine guns were firing in support of the assault units, their heavy explosive projectiles arcing in from the four points of the compass. Red tracer rounds from light machine guns streaked toward the Marine position, pointing the direction for reinforcements gathering in the valley. 60mm mortar shells smashed down and added rock splinters to the metal shrapnel whining through the air.

The North Vietnamese followed up the grenade shower with a full, well-coordinated assault, directed and controlled by shrill whistles and the clacking of bamboo sticks. From different directions, they rushed the position at the same time, firing automatic weapons, throwing grenades, and screaming. Howard later said he hadn't been sure how his troops would react. They were young and the situation looked hopeless. They had been shocked and confused by the ferocity of the attack and the screams of their own wounded.

But they reacted savagely. The first lines of enemy skirmishers were cut down seconds after they stood up and exposed themselves. The assault failed to gain momentum anyplace and the North Vietnamese in the rearward ranks had more sense than to copy the mistakes of the dead. Having failed in their swift charge, they went to earth and probed the perimeter, seeking a weak spot through which they could drive. To do this, small bands of the enemy tried to crawl quite close to a Marine, then overwhelm him with a burst of fire and several grenades.

But the Marines too used grenades and the American hand grenade contains twice the blast and shrapnel effect of the Chinese Communist stick grenade. The Marines could throw farther and more accurately than the enemy. A Marine would listen for a moment, gauge the direction and distance, pull the pin, and throw. High-pitched howls and excited jabberings mingled with the blasts. The North Vietnamese pulled back to regroup.

Howard had taken the PRC–25 radio from one of his communicators, Corporal Robert Lewis Martinez, and during the lull contacted Captain Geraghty and Lieutenant Colonel Sullivan. With his escape route cut off and his force facing overwhelming odds, Howard kept his message simple. "You've gotta get us out of here," he said. "There are too many of them for my people."

Sullivan tried. Because of his insistence upon detailed preplanning of extraction and fire support contingencies, he was a well-known figure at the Direct Air Support Center of the 1st Marine Division and when he called near midnight, he did not bandy words. He wanted flare ships, helicopters, and fixed-wing aircraft dispatched immediately to Nui Vu.

Somehow, the response was delayed. And shortly after midnight, the enemy forces gathered and rushed forward in strength a second time. The Marines threw the last of their grenades and fired their rifles semiautomatically, relying on accuracy to suppress volume. It did and the enemy fell back, but by that time every Marine had been wounded.

The living took the ammunition of the dead and lay under a moonless sky, wondering about the next assault. Although he did not tell anyone,

Howard doubted they could repel a massed charge by a determined enemy. From combat experience he knew too that the enemy, having been badly mauled twice, would listen for sounds which would indicate his force had been shattered or demoralized before surging forward again. Already up the slopes were floating the high, singsong taunts Marines had heard at other places in other wars. Voices which screeched: "Marines—you die tonight!" and "Marines, you die in an hour!"

Members of the platoon wanted to return the compliments. "Sure," said Howard, "go ahead and yell anything you want." And the Marines shouted back down the slopes all the curses and invectives they could remember from their collective repertoire. . . .

The North Vietnamese did not mount a third major attack and at 0100 an Air Force flare ship, with the poetic call sign of "Smoky Gold," came on station overhead. Howard talked to the pilot through his radio and the plane dropped its first flare. The mountainside was lit up. The Marines looked down the slopes. Lance Corporal Ralph Glober Victor stared, then muttered: "Oh my God, look at them." The others weren't sure it wasn't a prayer. North Vietnamese reinforcements filled the valley. Twenty-year-old Private First Class Joseph Kosoglow described it vividly: "There were so many, it was just like an anthill ripped apart. They were all over the place."

They shouldn't have been. Circling above the mountain were attack jets and armed helicopters. With growing frustration, they had talked to Howard but could not dive to the attack without light. Now they had light.

They swarmed in. The jets first concentrated on the valley floor and the approaches to Nui Vu, loosing rockets which hissed down and blanketed large areas. Then those fast, dangerous helicopters—the Hueys—scoured the slopes. At altitudes as low as twenty feet, they skimmed the brush, firing their machine guns in long, sweeping bursts. The Hueys pulled off to spot the jets, and again the planes dipped down, releasing bombs and napalm. Then the Hueys scurried back to pick off stragglers, survey the damage, and direct another run. One of the platoon's communicators, Corporal Martinez, said it in two sentences: "The Hueys were all over the place. The jets blocked the Viet Cong off."

Two Hueys stayed over Howard's position all night; when one helicopter had to return to home base and refuel, another would be sent out. The Huey pilots, Captain John M. Shields and Captain James M. Perryman, Jr., performed dual roles—they were the Tactical Air Controllers' Airborne (TACAs) who directed the bomb runs of the jets and they themselves strafed the enemy. The North Vietnamese tried unsuccessfully to shoot the helicopters down and did hit two out of the four Hueys alternating on station.

By the light of the flares, the jet pilots could see the hill mass and distinguish prominent terrain features but could not spot Howard's perimeter. To mark specific targets for the jets, the TACAs directed "Smoky" to drop flares right on the ground as signal lights and then called the jets down to pulverize the spot. Howard identified his position by flicking a refiltered flashlight on and off, and, guiding on that mark, the Huey pilots strafed within twenty-five meters of the Marines.

Still on the perimeter itself the fight continued. In the shifting light of the flares, the pilots were fearful of hitting the Marines and had to leave some space unexposed to fire in front of the Marines' lines. Into this space crawled the North Vietnamese.

For the Marines it was a war of hide and seek. Having run out of grenades, they had to rely on cunning and marksmanship to beat the attackers. Howard had passed the word to fire only at an identified target—and then only one shot at a time. The enemy fired all automatic weapons; the Marines replied with single shots. The enemy hurled grenades; the Marines threw back rocks.

It was a good tactic. A Marine would hear a noise and toss a rock in that general direction. The North Vietnamese would think it was a grenade falling and dive for another position. The Marine would roll or crawl low to a spot from which he could sight in on the position, and wait. In a few seconds, the North Vietnamese would raise his head to see why the grenade had not exploded. The Marine would fire one round. The range was generally less than thirty feet.

The accuracy of this fire saved the life of Corpsman Holmes. When he regained consciousness after a grenade had knocked him out, he saw a North Vietnamese dragging away the dead Marine beside him. Then another enemy reached over and grasped him by the cartridge belt. The soldier tugged at him.

Lance Corporal Victor was lying on his stomach behind a rock. He had been hit twice by grenades since the first flare had gone off and could scarcely move. He saw an enemy soldier bending over a fallen Marine. He sighted in and fired. The man fell backward. He saw a second enemy tugging at another Marine's body. He sighted in again and fired.

Shot between the eyes, the North Vietnamese slumped dead across Billie Holmes's chest. He pushed the body away and crawled back to the Marines' lines. His left arm was lanced with shrapnel, and his face was swollen and his head ringing from the concussion of the grenade. For the rest of the night, he crawled from position to position, bandaging and encouraging the wounded, and between times firing at the enemy.

Occasionally the flares would flicker out and the planes would have to break off contact to avoid crashing. In those instances, artillery under the control of the Special Forces and manned by Vietnamese gun crews would fill in the gap and punish any enemy force gathering at the base of Nui Vu.

"Stiff Balls," Howard had radioed the Special Forces camp at Hoi An, three miles south. "If you keep Charlie from sending another company up here, I'll keep these guys out of my position."

"Roger, Carnival Time." Captain Louis Maris, of the Army Special Forces, had replied, using Howard's own peculiar call sign. Both sides kept their parts of the bargain and the South Vietnamese crews who manned the 105mm howitzers threw in concentration after concentration of accurate artillery shells.

"Howard was talking on the radio. He was cool," Captain John Blair, the Special Forces commanding officer, recalled afterwards. "He stayed calm all the way through that night. But," he chuckled, "he never did get our call sign right!"

In the periods of darkness, each Marine fought alone. How some of them died no one knows. But the relieving force hours later found one Marine lying propped up against a rock. In front of him lay a dead enemy soldier. The muzzles of their weapons were touching each others' chests. Two Marine entrenching tools were recovered near a group of mangled North Vietnamese; both shovels were covered with blood. One Marine was crumpled beneath a dead enemy. Beside him lay another Vietnamese. The Marine was bandaged around the chest and head. His hand still clasped the hilt of a knife buried in the back of the soldier on top of him.

At 0300, a flight of H34 helicopters whirled over Nui Vu and came in to extract the platoon. So intense was the fire they met that they were unable to land and Howard was told he would have to fight on until dawn. Shortly thereafter, a ricochet struck Howard in the back. His voice over the radio faltered and died out. Those listening—the Special Forces personnel, the pilots, the high-ranking officers of the 1st Marine Division at Chulai—all thought the end had come. Then Howard's voice came back strong. Fearing the drowsing effect morphine can have, he refused to let Holmes administer the drug to ease the pain. Unable to use his legs, he pulled himself from hole to hole encouraging his men and directing their fire. Wherever he went, he dragged their lifeline—the radio.

Binns, the man whose shot had triggered the battle, was doing likewise. Despite severe wounds, he crawled around the perimeter, urging his men to conserve their ammunition, gathering enemy weapons and grenades for the Marines' use, giving assistance wherever needed.

None of the Marines kept track of the time. "I'll tell you this," said Howard, "you know that movie—*The Longest Day?* Well, compared to our night on the hill, *The Longest Day* was just a twinkle in the eye." But the longest night did pass and dawn came. Howard heralded its arrival. At 0525 he shouted, "O.K., you people, reveille goes in thirty-five minutes." At exactly 0600, his voice pealed out, "Reveille, reveille!" It was the start of another day and the perimeter had held.

On all sides of their position, the Marines saw enemy bodies and equipment. The North Vietnamese would normally have raked the battlefield clean but so deadly was the Marine fire that they left unclaimed many of those who fell close to the perimeter.

The firing had slacked off. Although badly mauled themselves, the enemy still had the Marines ringed in and did not intend to leave. Nor did haste make them foolhardy. They knew what the jets and the Hueys and the artillery and the Marine sharpshooting would do to them on the bare slopes in daylight. They slipped into holes and waited, intending to attack with more troops the next night.

Bursts of fire from light machine guns chipped the rocks above the Marines' heads. Firing uphill from concealed foxholes, the enemy could cut down any Marine who raised up and silhouetted himself against the skyline. Two of the .50-caliber machine guns were still firing sporadically.

There came a lull in the firing. A Huey buzzed low over the hillcrest, while another gunship hovered to one side, ready to pounce if the enemy took the bait. No one fired. The pilot, Major William J. Goodsell, decided to mark the position for a medical evacuation by helicopter. His Huey fluttered slowly down and hovered. Howard thought the maneuver too risky and said so. But Goodsell had run the risk and come in anyway. He dropped a smoke grenade. Still no fire. He waved to the relieved Howard and skimmed north over the forward slope, only ten feet above the ground.

The noise of machine guns drowned out the sound of the helicopter's engines. Tracers flew toward the Huey from all directions. The helicopter rocked and veered sharply to the right and zigzagged down the mountain. The copilot, First Lieutenant Stephen Butler, grabbed the stick and brought the crippled helicopter under control, crash landing in a rice paddy several miles to the east. The pilots were picked up by their wingman. But Major Goodsell, who had commanded Squadron VMO–6 for less than one week, died of gunshot wounds before they reached the hospital.

The medical pickup helicopter did not hesitate. It came in. Frantically, Howard waved it off. He was not going to see another shot down. The pilots were dauntless but not invulnerable. The pilot saw Howard's signal and turned off, bullets clanging off the armor plating of the undercarriage. Howard would wait for the infantry.

In anger, the jets and the Hueys now attacked the enemy positions anew. Flying lower and lower, they crisscrossed the slopes, searching for the machine-gun emplacements, offering themselves as targets, daring the enemy to shoot.

The enemy did. Another Huey was hit and crashed, its crew chief killed. The .50-calibers exposed their position and were silenced. Still the North Vietnamese held their ground. Perhaps the assault company, with all its automatic weapons and fresh young troops, had been ordered to wipe out the few Marines at any cost; perhaps the commanding officer had been killed and his subordinates were following dead orders; perhaps the enemy thought victory yet possible.

But then the Marine infantry came in. They had flown out at dawn but so intense was the enemy fire around Nui Vu, the helicopters had to circle for forty-five minutes while jets and artillery blasted a secure landing zone. During that time, First Lieutenant Richard E. Moser, a H34 helicopter pilot, monitored Howard's frequency and later reported: "It was something you'd read in a novel. His call sign was Carnival Time and he kept talking about these North Vietnamese down in holes in front of him. He'd say, 'You've gotta get this guy in the crater because he's hurting my boys.' He was really impressive. His whole concern was for his men."

On the southern slope of the mountain, helicopters finally dropped Charlie Company of the 5th Marines. The relief company climbed fast, ignoring sniper fire and wiping out small pockets of resistance. With the very first round they fired, the Marine 60mm mortar team knocked out the enemy mortar. Sergeant Frank Riojas, the weapons platoon commander, cut down a sniper at five hundred yards with a tracer round from his M14. Marine machine-gun sections were detached from the main body and sent up the steep fingers along the flanks of the hill to support by fire the company's movement. The North Vietnamese were now the hunted, as Marines scrambled around as well as up the slope, attempting to pinch off the enemy before they could flee.

The main column climbed straight upward. While yet a quarter of a mile away, the point man saw Howard's position on the plateau. The boulder which served as Howard's command post was the most prominent terrain feature on the peak. The platoon hurried forward. They had to step over enemy bodies to enter the perimeter. Howard's men had eight rounds of ammunition left.

"Get down," were Howard's first words of welcome. "There are snipers right in front of us." Another recon man shouted: "Hey, you got any cigarettes?" A cry went up along the line—not expressions of joy—but requests for cigarettes.

It was not that Howard's Marines were not glad to see other infantrymen; it was just that they had expected them. Staff Sergeant Richard Sullivan, who was with the first platoon to reach the recon Marines, said later: "One man told me he never expected to see the sun rise. But once it did, he knew we'd be coming."

The fight was not over. Before noon, in the hot daylight, despite artillery and planes firing in support, four more Marines would die.

At Howard's urging, Second Lieutenant Ronald Meyer quickly deployed his platoon along the crest. Meyer had graduated from the Naval Academy the previous June and intended to make the Marine Corps his career. He had spent a month with his bride before leaving for Vietnam. In the field he wore no shiny bars, and officers and men alike called him "Stump," because of his short, muscular physique.

Howard had assumed he was a corporal or a sergeant and was shouting orders to him. Respecting Howard's knowledge and performance, Meyer obeyed. He never did mention his rank. So Staff Sergeant Howard, waving off offers of aid, proceeded to direct the tactical maneuvers of the relieving company, determined to wipe out the small enemy band dug in not twenty meters downslope.

Meyer hollered for members of his platoon to pass him grenades. He would then lob them downslope toward the snipers' holes. By peering around the base of the boulder, Howard was able to direct his throws. "A little more to the right on the next one, buddy. About five yards farther. That's right. No, a little too strong." The grenades had little effect and the snipers kept firing. Meyer shouted he wanted air on the target. The word was passed back for the air liaison officer to come forward. The platoon waited.

Lance Corporal Terry Redic wanted to fire his rifle grenade at the snipers. A tested sharpshooter, he had several kills to his credit. In small fire fights he often disdained to duck, preferring to suppress hostile fire by his own rapid accurate shooting. Meyer's way seemed too slow. He raised up, knelt on one knee, and sighted downslope looking for a target. He never found one. The enemy shot first and killed him instantly.

Meyer swore vehemently. "Let's get that __ __ __. You coming with me, Sotello?" "Yes, Stump." Lance Corporal David Sotello turned to get his rifle and some other men. Meyer didn't wait. He started forward with a grenade in each hand. "Keep your head down, buddy, they can shoot," yelled Howard.

Meyer crawled for several yards, then threw a grenade at a hole. It blasted an enemy solider. He turned, looking upslope. Another sniper shot him in the back. Sotello heard the shot as he started to crawl down.

So did Hospitalman 3d Class John Markillie, the platoon corpsman. He crawled toward the fallen lieutenant. "For God's sake, keep your head down!" yelled Howard. Markillie reached his lieutenant. He sat up to examine the wound. A sniper shot him in the chest.

Another corpsman, Holloday, and a squad leader, Corporal Melville, crawled forward. They could not feel Meyer's pulse. Markillie was still breathing. Ignoring the sniper fire, they began dragging and pushing his body up the hill.

Melville was hit in the head. He rolled over. His helmet bounced off. He shook his head and continued to crawl. The round had gone in one side of the helmet and ripped out the other, just nicking the corporal above his left ear. Melville and Holloday dragged Markillie into the perimeter.

From Chulai, the battalion commander called his company commander, First Lieutenant Marshall "Buck" Darling. "Is the landing zone secure, Buck?" "Well," a pause, ". . . not spectacularly." Back at the base two noncommissioned officers were listening. "I wonder what he meant by that?" asked the junior sergeant. "What the hell do you think it means, stupid?" replied the older sergeant. "He's getting shot at."

Ignoring his own wounds, Corpsman Billie Holmes was busy supervising the corpsmen from Charlie Company as they administered to the wounded. With the fire fight still going on to the front, helicopter evacuation was not possible from within the perimeter. The wounded had to be taken rearward to the south slope. Holmes roved back and forth, making sure that all of his buddies were accounted for and taken out.

The pilots had seen easier landing sites. "For the medical evacs," Moser said, "a pilot had to come in perpendicular to the ridge, then cock his bird around before he sat down. We could get both main mounts down —first—the—tail—well—sometimes we got it down. We were still taking fire."

Holmes reported that there was still one Marine, whom he had seen die, missing. Only after repeated reassurances that they would not leave without the body were the infantry able to convince him and Howard that it was time they too left. They helped the Navy corpsman and the Marine sergeant to a waiting helicopter. Howard's job was done.

Another had yet to be finished. There was a dead Marine to be found somewhere on the field of battle. But before a search could be conducted, the last of the enemy force had to be destroyed.

First Lieutenant Phil Freed flopped down beside Melville. Freed was the foreward air controller attached to Charlie Company that day. He had run the last quarter mile uphill when he heard Meyer needed air. With the rounds cracking near his head, he needed no briefing. He contacted two F8 Crusader jets circling overhead. "This is Cottage 14. Bring it on down on a dry run. This has to be real tight. Charlie is dug in right on our lines." At the controls of the jets were First Lieutenants Richard W. Deilke and Edward H. Menzer.

"There were an awful lot of planes in the air," Menzer said. "We didn't think we'd be used so we called DASC (Direct Air Support Center) and asked for another mission. We got diverted to the FAC (Forward Air Controller), Cottage 14. He told us he had a machine-gun nest right in front of him."

As they talked back and forth, Menzer thought he recognized Freed's voice. Later he learned he had indeed; Freed had flown jets with him in another squadron a year earlier.

Freed was lying in a pile of rocks on the military crest of the northern finger of the hill. Since he himself had flown the F8 Crusader, Freed could talk to the pilots in a language they understood. Still, he was not certain they could help. He didn't know whether they could come that close and still not hit the Marine infantrymen. On their first run, he deliberately called the jets in wide so he could judge the technical skills and precision of the pilots. Rock steady.

He called for them to attack in earnest. When they heard the target was twenty meters from the FAC, it was the pilots' turn to be worried. "As long as you're flying parallel to the people, it's O.K.," Menzer said. "Because it's a good shooting bird. But even so, I was leery at first to fire with troops that near."

Unknown to them, the two pilots were about to fly one of the closest direct air support missions in the history of fixed-wing aviation. They approached from the northeast with the sun behind them, and cut across the ridgeline parallel to the friendly lines. They strafed without room for error. The gunsight reflector plate in an F8 Crusader jet looks like a bull's-eye with the rings marked in successive 10-mil increments. When the pilots in turn aligned their sights while three thousand feet away, the target lay within the 10-mil ring and the Marine position was at the edge of the ring. The slightest variance of the controls would rake the Marine infantrymen with fire. In that fashion, each pilot made four strafing passes, skimming by ten to twenty feet above the ridge. Freed feared they would both crash, so close did their wings dip to the crest of the hill. The impact of the cannon shells showered the infantrymen with dirt. They swore they could tell the color of the pilot's eyes. In eight attacks, the jet pilots fired 350 20mm explosive shells into an area sixty meters long and ten to twenty meters wide. The hillside was gouged and torn, as if a bulldozer had churned back and forth across it.

Freed cautiously lifted his head. A round cracked by. One enemy had survived. Somebody shouted that the shot came from the position of the sniper who had killed Meyer. The lieutenant's body lay several yards downslope.

The F8 Crusaders had ample fuel left. Menzer called to say they could make dummy runs over the position if the Marines thought it would be useful. Freed asked them to try it.

The company commander, Buck Darling, watched the jets. As they passed, he noticed the firing stopped momentarily. The planes would be his cover. "I'm going to get Stump. Coming, Brown?" he asked the nearest Marine.

Lance Corporal James Brown was not a billboard Marine. His offbeat sense of humor often conflicted with his superiors' sense of duty. On the hill relieving the recon unit, however, Brown was all business. He emptied several rifle magazines and hurled grenade after grenade. When he ran out of grenades, he threw rocks to keep the snipers ducking. All the while he screamed and cursed, shouting every insult and blasphemy he could think of. Howard had been very impressed, both with Brown's actions and with his vocabulary.

He was not out of words when Darling asked him to go after Meyer's body. As they crawled over the crest, Brown tugged at his company commander's boot. "Don't sweat it, Lieutenant, they can only kill us." Darling did not reply. They reached Meyer's body and tried to pull it back while crawling on their stomachs. They lacked the strength.

"All right, let's carry him," said Darling. It was Brown's turn to be speechless. He knew what had happened to every Marine on the slope who had raised his head—and here was his officer suggesting they stand straight up! "We'll time our moves with the jets." When the jets passed low, they stumbled and scrambled forward a few yards with the burden, then flattened out as the jets pulled up. The sniper snapped shots at them after every pass. Bullets chipped the rocks around them. They had less than thirty feet to climb. It took over a dozen rushes. When they rolled over the crest they were exhausted. Only the enemy was left on the slope.

The infantry went after him. Corporal Samuel Roth led his eight-man squad around the left side of the slope. On the right, Sergeant Riojas set a machine gun up on the crest to cover the squad. A burst of automatic fire struck the tripod of the machine gun. A strange duel developed. The sniper would fire at the machine gun. His low position enabled him to aim in exactly on the gun. The Marines would duck until he fired, then reach up and loose a burst downhill, forcing the sniper to duck.

With the firing, the sniper could not hear the squad crashing through the brush on his right side. Roth brought his men on line facing toward the sniper. With fixed bayonets they began walking forward. They could see no movement in the clumps of grass and torn earth.

There was a lull in the firing. The sniper heard the squad, turned and fired. Bullets whipped by the Marines. Roth's helmet spun off. He fell. The other Marines flopped to the ground. Roth was uninjured. The steel helmet had saved a second Marine's life within an hour. He was not even aware that his helmet had been shot off. "When I give the word, kneel and fire," he said. "Now!" The Marines rose and their rounds kicked up dust and clumps of earth in front of them. They missed the sniper. He had ducked into his hole. The Marines lay back down. Roth swore. "All right—put in fresh magazines and let's do it again. Now!"

Just as the Marines rose, the sniper bobbed up like a duck in a shooting gallery. A bullet knocked him backwards against the side of his hole. Roth charged, the other Marines sprinting behind him. He drove forward with his bayonet. A grenade with the release pin intact rolled from the sniper's left hand. Roth jerked the blade back. The sniper slumped forward over his machine gun.

The hill was quiet. It was noon. Darling declared the objective secure. In the tall grass in front of Riojas' machine gun, the infantrymen found the body of the missing Marine. The Marines paused to search thirty-nine enemy dead for documents, picked up eighteen automatic weapons (most of them Chinese), climbed on board a flight of helicopters, and flew off the plateau.

Of the eighteen Marines in the reconnaissance platoon, six were killed; the other twelve were wounded. Every Marine under Howard's command received the Purple Heart. Fifteen were recommended for the Silver Star; Binns and Holmes were nominated for the Navy Cross; Howard was recommended for the Medal of Honor.

If the action had centered around just one man, then it could be considered a unique incident of exceptional bravery on the part of an exceptional man. It is that. But perhaps it is something more. Few would notice anything unique about the 1st Reconnaissance Platoon of Charlie Company. Just in reading the names of its dead, one has the feeling that here are the typical and the average, who, well trained and well led, rose above normal expectations to perform an exemplary feat of arms: John Adams, Ignatius Carlisi, Thomas Glawe, James McKinney, Alcadio Mascarenas, Jerrald Thompson. (Adapted from *Small Unit Action in Vietnam, Summer 1966,* by Captain Francis J. West, Jr., USMCR. Originally published in 1967 by Historical Branch of the Marine Corps, reprinted by Arno Press, 1967.)

6 Putting Skill, Will, and Teamwork Together

Here in this short chapter, we'll take what we've just discussed about teamwork, pull all of it together, and combine it with what we talked about in the chapter "How to Develop Soldiers." What this will give you is a small-unit leader's *concept of operation* for combining SKILL, WILL, and TEAMWORK all together into a single unit—your unit.

First off, review in your mind the things we said about building SKILL and building WILL and building TEAMWORK. What can you remember about each of those critical subjects?

Next, think about all the teams or crews you've ever been a part of since you came into the Army. Pick the one you remember best. A good one or a sorry one. If you want to, pick the one you lead right now. Whatever team you pick, if you think about it a little while, it will fit pretty well into one of four categories. The fit won't be *precise,* but there will be a *best* fit—just as when we fitted individuals into the four categories of the "able and willing" scale. A team will be harder to categorize than a man because you have to think about the team as a *whole* and not about any individual parts. Whatever team you have in mind, it's going to fit pretty well into one of the following four:

LOW SKILL, LOW WILL, LOW TEAMWORK
HIGH SKILL, LOW WILL, LOW TEAMWORK
HIGH SKILL, HIGH WILL, LOW TEAMWORK
HIGH SKILL, HIGH WILL, HIGH TEAMWORK

In a moment, we will describe each one of those four kinds of teams in detail. We'll tell you what probably caused it to be the way it is; what "indicators" you can see for each kind; and what you, as a leader, should do in each case. But for right now, look just at the list of the four categories. Again, you need to get the "big picture."

From top to bottom, you can see that those teams get better and better. You can see stages in the development of a team, ending up with the kind that has the best chance to survive and win on the battlefield. Leadership is what moves a team through the stages. It works for the fire-team leader building a team out of individuals, and it works for the squad leader building a squad *team* out of two fire teams, and so on up the chain.

If you look at the first category, you can see that there's going to be a lot of work, a lot of time, and a lot of tasks that leaders won't get accomplished. If you look at the last category, you can see well-trained individuals in high-performing crews in a highly effective *unit*. The last category is your goal. It is achieved when the leadership of the unit gets SKILL, WILL, and TEAMWORK *put together right.*

There is a "best way to lead" for each of the four categories. The way to lead must be tailored to the kind of team. The first kind of team is obviously going to need detailed instruction and close supervision that is "agile, mobile, and hostile." The fourth kind needs mission-type orders, general supervision, and trust. It should be easy to see what will happen if you give mission-type orders to the kind of team characterized by low skill, low will, and low teamwork. As we've said so many times before, much of the effectiveness of leadership depends on being able to apply "different strokes for different folks."

In order to tailor the way you lead to the kind of team you're leading, you need to be able to, first, identify which one of the four kinds of team you have to work with and, second, be able to do the right leadership thing for that particular kind of team. In the four descriptions below, we'll start with the toughest kind of team and move you on toward the kind we need on the battlefield. Most of the discussion is aimed at the company commander, but with a little adjustment, the techniques and tricks of the trade will work for any leader who's trying to "train his men as a team."

YOUR TEAM: LOW SKILL, LOW WILL, LOW TEAMWORK?

This kind of team isn't necessarily "bad." You were a member of this kind of team when you first came into the Army. During the first few days of

Basic Training, very few men had any military skill at all; individual "motivation" for being in the Army went every which way; and the leadership of the unit hadn't had time to train men to work *together.* This same kind of team can exist out in line units, especially when there has been a major mission change with not enough planning and direction from the leadership (lack of "vertical teamwork") or when the unit has experienced a prolonged period of operating under poor, inconsistent leadership.

Indicators:
- Poor SQT performance by a large number of soldiers.
- Low numbers of subtasks completed on last ARTEP.
- High rates of Article 15, C/M, and AWOL.
- Large number of early discharges.
- Low level of physical fitness.
- *Extremely* low reenlistment rate among first-termers.
- Low reenlistment rates for career NCOs.
- Poor overall personal appearance of individual soldiers.
- Equipment missing, poorly maintained, or not "signed for."
- Unit area and billets poorly maintained.
- Large volume of complaints about the unit.
- Absences from scheduled training.

Best Way to Lead:

- Focus on building individual skill, and do it through the NCOs. Give them time, resources, instructions, supervision, and critique.
- To start:

  Call all NCOs together. (*Don't* assume there's something wrong with them. *Do* assume they don't know very well what's expected of them, i.e., what their responsibilities are.)

  Describe in detail the problems detected and the standards expected.

  Establish *individual skill* as first priority.

  Explain that individual skills is "sergeants' business."

  Direct each leader to "inventory" the individual skills of each individual he's responsible for and come up with a plan for making up shortages. This includes any individuals on "SD."
- Schedule as much available time for individual skill training as possible. Push *integrated* individual skill training. Reward NCOs who work out their own informal "systems" for good integrated training. Many of them will.

113

- Find the training resources that the NCOs need. Check individual training daily. Check Soldier's Manuals and Job Books.
- Set successive goals for percentage of individual skills to be trained. Don't let up. Get 60 percent, then go for 70 percent, then 80 percent. When you get to around 95 percent, maybe you can slack off—a little.
- When indicators begin to disappear and the NCOs have individual skill levels moving upward, begin to shift to the next "way to lead."

YOUR TEAM: *HIGH* SKILL, LOW WILL, LOW TEAMWORK?

This kind of team has a successful individual training program, but the drive to build individual skills has resulted in the leadership giving a lower priority to the welfare of the soldiers. *Mission* and *men* are out of balance. There hasn't been enough concern about individual needs, and not enough time and effort spent taking care of these needs.

Indicators:

- High SQT scores.
- Hard work on individual skills, *when* NCOs are supervising.
- Low number of subtasks completed on last ARTEP.
- Many hours dedicated to individual training during recent training weeks.
- Poor performance by soldiers in the absence of leaders.
- High Article 15 rate and frequent use of other punishment.
- Higher than normal frequency of inspections and "pre-inspections."
- High volume of criticism directed at unit-level leaders.
- Little mutual help and assistance among NCOs and, therefore, among the soldiers also.
- Installation-level emphasis on making things *look* good rather than *work* good.

Best Way to Lead:

- Focus on building *will* and, again, do it through the noncommissioned officers.
- To start:
  Call all NCOs together.
  Tell them they're getting good at individual training, and the better they get, the less effort it takes. Therefore, there's some "spare" effort available.

Have them double their effort on just two things: (1) *rewarding* good performance and (2) keeping their men *informed,* especially about *why* they are required to perform certain tasks. *No* excuse making, just straight-out explanations.

- Start a drive to get the chain of command to *delegate* twice as much. You set the example and begin by delegating twice as many tasks to *your* able and willing subordinate leaders. Push this all the way down the chain until you see fire-team leaders delegating to able and willing soldiers.

- Open up more opportunities for soldiers and leaders to contribute to the *unit.* Give them opportunities to *volunteer* to assume extra responsibilities, work on certain *unit* projects, make suggestions, and so on. Avoid a routine, scheduled "open door policy," but work these contributions up through the chain so the leadership of the unit will know what's happening.

- Work up a FIVE-PARAGRAPH FIELD ORDER directed to the mission of upgrading the unit's working and living conditions. Include eight to ten small-unit projects with specific target dates for each. NCOs execute; officers support. Special attention to Mess Hall, billets, and families.

- Analyze existing athletic and off-duty recreational programs—not just what facilities are available, but how many troops know about them and how many troops use them, and when. Double the emphasis given to these programs.

- When the negative indicators begin to disappear and you start seeing numerous cases of soldiers doing *good* work without close supervision, begin to shift up to the next "way to lead."

YOUR TEAM: *HIGH* SKILL, *HIGH* WILL, LOW TEAMWORK?

This kind of team is *caused* by unit leadership that is able to develop an effective individual skills training program *and,* at the same time, knows and meets the individual needs of the soldiers. If you had good, competent leadership in Basic Training, you were in this kind of team at about graduation time. Many teams in line units today are of this kind. This kind of team looks good and is good, but it's a long way from being ready to *fight.*

Indicators:

- High SQT scores.
- Low number of subtasks completed in last ARTEP.

- Large number of positive comments from troops about squad and platoon level leadership. (Some negative comments about leadership at company level and above will still continue.)
- High level of individual personal appearance.
- High reenlistment rates among first-termers *and* NCOs.
- Inconsistent quality in performance of *team* tasks.
- Willing, but poorly coordinated, performance, confusion among soldiers when leaders aren't around.
- High level of physical fitness.
- Individual equipment all on hand and maintained.
- Equipment and supplies used by more than one soldier are apt to be missing, inoperable, or poorly maintained.

Best Way to Lead:

- Focus on building teams—"horizontal" teams (among squad leaders, for example) and "vertical" teams (among the links in the chain of command).
- To start:

  Call *all* subordinate leaders together, both commissioned and noncommissioned.

  Emphasize the *continuing* importance of what the leadership of the unit is already doing almost automatically—effective individual skill training and a high frequency of *rewarding* individuals for doing the right things the right way.

  Explain that the overall unit leadership emphasis is now shifting to collective (team) tasks, with all leaders to put heavy emphasis on the how-to's for building teams.

  Lay out the overall leadership strategy for "vertical teamwork" between NCOs and officers. *NCOs:* You *maintain* the good systems already developed for training individual skills and taking care of the needs of the soldiers. Officers support this effort with scheduling resources and supervision. *Officers:* You now lead the "main attack" for the leadership of this unit. Collective tasks and DRILLS are *your* primary responsibility. NCOs support this effort by keeping individual skill levels maintained and by building the basic fire *teams,* crew *teams,* and squad *teams* that the officers need to work with.

- Schedule DRILL (of all kinds), beginning at squad level, wherever and whenever the training schedule and any available open time will permit.
- Train and critique company officers in ARTEP subtasks and techniques of effective DRILL.
- Provide training time wherein company officers can plan and conduct the kind of DRILL *they* feel their teams require.

- When the negative indicators begin to disappear and when squads and platoons begin to run small-unit battle drills smoothly with a minimum of shouting and confusion, begin to shift up to the final "way to lead."

YOUR TEAM: *HIGH* SKILL, *HIGH* WILL, *HIGH* TEAMWORK!

This last kind of team, which is your goal, is achieved by unit leadership which has learned, itself, how to work as a *team* in putting together SKILL, WILL, and TEAMWORK. If you've ever been in a unit where everyone believed that each man and every crew was highly trained, and that all belonged to a solid, firm, confident, well-trained outfit that knew where it was going and what it had to do, then you've been in this finest kind of team. Some companies in our Army are like this today. And so are some platoons, and some squads, and some fire teams. *All* of them *can* be.

Indicators:

- SQT scores will continue to be high.
- High rate of subtasks completed on last ARTEP.
- Barracks thefts and crimes against each other down to almost zero.
- Very few comments critical of the leadership at any level in the unit. Leadership above company sometimes questioned, but seldom considered.
- Individual and crew-served weapons and equipment maintained in a high state of readiness.
- Unit area well maintained and policed *all* the time.
- Individual soldiers usually do the right things, the right way, on their own, without being told by leaders.
- Individual soldiers frequently police each other's performance and behavior.
- Soldiers *and* leaders usually use the words "us" and "we" and "our" when they're talking about the unit.
- The traditional "command indicators" by which *whole* units are often judged are high and are becoming part of the unit's "reputation."
- In addition to all the traditional indicators of a combat-ready team, there are some nontraditional indicators which you'll start to see as a unit begins to "get it all together":
  There will be "rhythm of operation" in the way the team operates in the field during a battle DRILL. All actions of the team and the leaders seem

117

to go "right," especially at times when they would usually go wrong. The team pulls off extremely difficult and complicated tasks with what others might call "luck," but the team is "lucky" time and time again, even during a night relief.

When a new soldier joins the team, he won't be accepted automatically. He'll have to *earn* membership in the team. The team will check him out, mostly on his military skill. When the team sees he's *trying* and *learning,* they'll accept him as a "pro."

The team will have its own "history," and the team members will talk about it. This "history" won't cover what the team did in WWII, but the team members will have a collection of stories about themselves ("us" and "we") stretching back maybe a year. Most of those stories will be peacetime "war stories" about what the team or particular members of the team did *out in the field.*

The team will begin to develop its own private "language," with nicknames for each other and for weapons and pieces of equipment. Outsiders may not understand this "language," but inside the team, the words and gestures are quick shortcuts to rapid communication about "what to do next."

The team will often mix maintenance of weapons and equipment right in with active battle drill performance. Short breaks in the action will find team members, on their own, cleaning this and adjusting that.

Many times, the team will get its tasks accomplished in a way far different from "what the book says." They will meet and usually exceed any established standards, but they'll often invent their own way of how to do it.

Best Way to Lead:

This kind of high-performing team is the living criteria of what a combat-ready team should be. It got that way through the investment of countless hours of leadership *planning* and hard work by the leadership of the unit. At this point, SKILL, WILL, and TEAMWORK have been *put together.* And *balanced.* This kind of team needs only four things:

- Mission-type orders.
- General supervision.
- Trust.
- . . . and a battlefield.

7 Leadership Skills

This final chapter is a carefully selected tool kit of all-purpose leadership skills. They provide solid, commonsense guidelines for you to use. More importantly, each is an outline for a half hour's worth of teaching when you are developing the skills of those young leaders below you.

These are quality tools, designed for the company-level leader. They've all been tested. They all *work*. They help solve leadership problems. And in this great big Army of ours, there are approximately 1,823,642 different kinds of leadership problems.

Fitting the tools to the problems is *your* responsibility, Captain, Lieutenant, Sergeant. Use them to handle all the good, tough challenges you and your young leaders are going to meet in the difficult tasks of building SKILL and building WILL and building TEAMWORK, and putting all these together to WIN on the BATTLEFIELD.

HOW TO

- Listen
- Process Information
- Transmit
- Be a Self-starter
- Plan
- Manage Time
- Make Meetings Work

- Set Standards
- Delegate
- Inspect
- Maintain Good Performance Levels
- Provide Corrective Feedback to a Soldier

119

- Reward Individuals
- Bring Smoke
- Handle a "Sharpshooter"
- Counsel
- Use the EER and OER to Improve Performance
- Check Unit Performance
- Provide Feedback to Teams

- Use Team Rewards
- Use Team Punishment
- Motivate
- Prepare for Stress
- Handle Fear on the Battlefield
- Build a Winning Attitude
- Supervise
- Ask the Right Questions

HOW TO LISTEN

One basic responsibility of the leader is the development, adjustment, and orientation of individual soldiers. The leader should strive to develop subordinate potential, delegate responsibility, and achieve cooperation. To do so he must have, among other abilities, the ability to listen effectively. The most effective kind of listening is called "active listening." It's called that because the listener has to *work hard* at listening. When soldiers are listened to carefully, they will *talk* more carefully and will try to make clear exactly what they are feeling and thinking. The best way to get soldiers to listen carefully to you is to SET THE EXAMPLE; listen carefully to *them.*

When to Do It

- Whenever someone else is talking to you.

How to Do It

- Listen for total meaning—both the content of the message and any emotion associated with the message (e.g., anger, fear, happiness). Listen for both *what* a person says and *how* he says it.
- If it looks as though someone is so emotional that he is having trouble communicating with you, then tell him about it (e.g., "Calm down, soldier—you aren't making sense").
- Test your understanding of the message. For example, while you're listening, ask yourself every now and then, "Could I repeat or restate what he just said?"
- Listen to *yourself* while you're listening. If you're getting angry or excited *inside,* chances are you're not hearing the other man very accurately.

How to Know When It's Done Right

- You begin to see your soldiers listening to *you* more carefully.
- In situations where you have to pass on information, you don't overlook things.
- More soldiers want to talk with you.

HOW TO PROCESS INFORMATION

We all know how critical communication is to success on the battlefield. Because it is so critical, there have been great advances in communications technology in recent years. With the aid of modern electronic equipment, it is now possible to send, receive, and store large amounts of information at incredible speed. But quantity, speed, and coverage are *not* the only requirements of communication. It is also important that we communicate clearly and precisely. *Much* information passes through leaders because they *are* leaders. There are some simple rules that can lead to greater understanding of the *meaning* of a message.

When to Do It

- Whenever you receive information from someone else.

How to Do It

- Pay attention to what is going on around you. Knowing as much as you can about "the big picture," as well as "what's going on" in the unit, will help you better understand all kinds of information that you receive.
- If you think you need to recall something later on, then *write it down in your notebook.* A leader should never be without a notebook and pencil.
- Note the conditions that created the information. The number of rumors just about triples when there is a lot of uncertainty, fear, or stress in the situation.
- Consider the source from which you're getting information. Remember that soldiers come from different backgrounds. Phrases and actions can mean different things to different people.
- Look for signs that emotions are affecting the soldiers who are bringing you information (e.g., nervousness, anger, fright).
- Continually ask yourself, "What is the soldier *trying* to tell me?"

- Get in the habit of always asking questions about what your soldiers tell you.

How to Know When It's Done Right

- When you can tell the other person, in your own words, what *you* think he said to you, and the two of you agree.

HOW TO TRANSMIT

Effective communication is an absolute must if our Army is to accomplish its mission. In a way, "Leadership = Communication," because about 80 percent of a leader's time is spent in some form of communication. The leader, as he "influences" soldiers to accomplish a mission, has only one real tool: information. He does not "handle" soldiers. He motivates, guides, and organizes them to do their own work. He does this with the *information* he has. His primary tool to do all of this is the spoken or written word.

The guidelines below will help "senders," like you, put together messages that will be received accurately by most soldiers of average interest, motivation, and ability.

When to Do It

- Whenever you send a message to someone, spoken *or* written.

How to Do It

- Make the message as simple as possible. Start with a clear, simple statement of the purpose of the message. Don't overload the message with unnecessary information.
- Organize the message in a way that is easily understood by the *receiver*. One of the keys to this is KNOWING YOUR MEN.
- State the message in soldier language. Avoid "official" jargon and long-winded words.
- Use an example to illustrate any major *new* point or idea.
- Draw pictures and sketches to go along with words whenever possible. Use a blackboard, a notebook, or a stick in the sand.
- Repeat the important points of a message at least twice.

- Summarize the major points of a message.
- *Ask* the receiver for feedback.
- When time permits, ask the receiver to repeat back or explain to you, in his own words, what you have just told him.

How to Know When It's Done Right

- When the receiver gives you feedback that tells you he understood the message.
- When the receiver behaves in accordance with the intent of the message; when you see him *do* what you had in mind when you *told* him what to do.

HOW TO BE A SELF-STARTER

On the battlefield our Army needs leaders who know when and how to take the initiative. Good leaders don't wait around for orders when something must be done to ensure successful mission performance. Good leaders recognize problems, and when appropriate, they take action to solve them. Initiative has made the difference in hundreds of our Army's past battles. In order to do it intelligently on today's battlefield, it needs to be practiced during training. Taking the initiative must be encouraged, even at the expense of acceptable mistakes. The wise leader learns from mistakes before the battle begins, not after. The good leader does everything he can to avoid mistakes before the battle, but mistakes will occur, and it is far less costly for each leader to make his mistakes *before* the battle.

When to Do It

- When there appears to be a method to perform your mission that is better than the method you are now using.

How to Do It

- Always keep your eyes and ears open. Look for better ways to perform your mission. Encourage your soldiers to do this also—and encourage them to let you know when they see a better way.
- Carefully evaluate each "better way" in terms of your mission. If it looks

like your "better way" will accomplish your mission more efficiently, then you have to check it out and get it coordinated.

- Continue performing your mission using the method already selected.
- Try to contact your superior to discuss the "better way."
- If you can contact your superior, explain your "better way" to him. Don't implement the "better way" if he says no.
- If you *cannot* contact your superior, ask yourself, Does this "better way" fit in terms of the understanding I have of my superior's concept of operation? If it doesn't, continue performing your mission in the manner directed.
- If the "better way" appears to fit in your superior's concept of the operation, compare the consequences of the method you are now using with the "better way."
- Be sure the "better way" *is* more effective and less costly. Don't use it just to show you have initiative or for the sake of being different.

How to Know When It's Done Right

- You begin to accomplish your missions using only a limited amount of your resources.
- Time, effort, materiel, supplies, seldom seem to be "wasted."

HOW TO PLAN

Leaders at all Army levels need to plan constantly for the future. THE ESTIMATE OF THE SITUATION is the best thinking tool for doing this, particularly on the battlefield. In addition to the ESTIMATE, there is another fairly simple planning guide that will help you get the right things done right, on a daily basis, even when some things go wrong.

When to Do It

- When you have been given a task or know that you have something to do even though no one has told you. In either case, you need a "plan."

How to Do It

- Determine whether you should develop the plan by yourself or get some subordinates involved. Does time permit you to involve others? Do others have the necessary skills and knowledge to assist you?

- List alternatives that you think might accomplish the task.
- Figure out the essential steps in each alternative.
- Put the steps in proper order.
- Determine *when* each step has to be finished.
- Pay close attention to any of the steps that your experience tells you could go wrong.
- ASSUME IT WILL GO WRONG.
- For each alternative way of accomplishing the task, develop a plan to cover things that could go wrong.

How to Know When It's Done Right

- When there is a reduction in the number of "last-minute" problems confronting your unit.
- When you can adjust quickly to change and errors without getting rattled.

HOW TO MANAGE TIME

Time is the most precious human resource. Once used, time can never be replaced. The most important decisions made by small-unit leaders involve the use of time: what the leader will be doing with his time and what the leader's soldiers will be doing with their time. A resource as critical as time must not be treated in a haphazard or careless manner. Use of time must be carefully planned—and managed.

When to Do It

- When you notice you and your soldiers are not getting tasks done on time according to your own expectations or the schedules you're supposed to meet.
- When you end up scheduled to do two or more things at the same time.
- When you seem to forget about performing some tasks until you are reminded—usually at the last minute.
- When your soldiers are complaining because things just don't seem "organized" to them—everyone seems to be running around like "chickens with their heads cut off."

How to Do It

- Buy or draw up a monthly calendar that gives you room to record scheduled activities on a daily basis (good calendars are normally available through your local supply system).

- Keep the calendar up to date at all times. When you learn about an important activity, record it as soon as you can on your calendar.

- Start a "things to do" notebook. The notebook should be small enough to fit in your pocket. Each time you are told to perform a task or you otherwise identify a task that must be performed, record the task and *when it must be completed* in this notebook. After you complete each task, cross out the entry in your notebook and record the time and date the task was completed.

- Set aside a specific time period each day to spend with your soldiers *regardless of other commitments.* Always spend this time with your soldiers unless a true emergency prevents you from doing it.

- Set aside a specific period of time each day to handle paperwork. Always work on your paperwork during this time unless a true emergency requires you to do something else.

- Establish time limits for meetings whenever possible. Schedule less important meetings immediately before other scheduled activities so you won't be tempted to let them run over.

- When a conflict for using your time develops, establish your priorities based on your missions. Activities that must be accomplished in order to prepare your soldiers and your unit for battle *must come first.*

- At least once a day, review your monthly calendar and your list of "things to do." This should normally be done in the morning. When you have a lot to do on a day, write out a list of "things to do today" and list them in order of their priority. Do them in that order.

- Be prepared and be willing to work the amount of time needed to accomplish your mission. DON'T PLAN YOUR ACTIVITIES AROUND AN EIGHT-HOUR DAY. PLAN YOUR DAY AROUND YOUR ACTIVITIES.

How to Know When It's Done Right

- All required tasks seem to be accomplished on time.
- Conflicts in your schedule don't occur.
- Things seem to run "smoothly."
- Soldiers aren't surprised when you ask them about tasks they are supposed to have done.

HOW TO MAKE MEETINGS WORK

Most of us attend meetings every day. Sometimes these meetings are designed to pass out information. Other times, they are used to get ideas on a particular problem. Regardless of their purpose, meetings take up a lot of valuable time and frequently do not accomplish what they are supposed to. Once you have determined that a meeting is the best communication tool, always follow these simple rules to make it as effective as possible.

When to Do It

- Whenever you decide a quicker way of communicating would not be good enough.
- Whenever a real need for a meeting is apparent.

How to Do It

- Call together *only* the necessary people.
- State the purpose of the meeting. Have an agenda, with major points, and tell the attendees about it ahead of time.
- Set a time limit. Any company-level meeting more than thirty minutes long is probably ineffective. One way to make meetings end on time is to schedule them thirty minutes before PT or some mandatory activity. Another way to keep them short is to have "stand-up" meetings with no chairs.
- Make a habit of starting meetings *precisely* on time. Embarrass anyone who comes late. Don't let him slip in and sit down in the rear.
- Don't permit interruptions. Tell attendees to hold their questions until end of meeting.
- *Stick to the subject.* Best way to do this is to write down the objective of the meeting, and the agenda, on a blackboard or piece of chart paper.
- When issues are to be *discussed,* make sure participants do their "homework" *ahead* of time.
- Don't let unresolved issues go unanswered. If it's a "one-man" issue, talk to that man *after the meeting.*
- Summarize what was covered in the meeting and who's going to do what.

- Write down the results of the meeting so people who didn't attend can find out what happened.
- Don't schedule meetings unless *you* think they are absolutely necessary. About half of the usual, scheduled, "routine" meetings are a waste of time.
- A twenty-minute meeting early in the morning is usually far more effective than a sixty-minute meeting late in the day.

How to Know When It's Done Right

- Participants show up on time and are prepared.
- Discussion focuses on the topic.
- Meeting adjourns on time.
- Meeting objectives are accomplished.

HOW TO SET STANDARDS

The best way to make sure that jobs and tasks are done right is to see to it that clear, precise standards are set. Soldiers work best when they know exactly what is expected of them. The most effective standards are those that are realistic, challenging, specific, measurable, and "do-able"—with a specific time deadline. In assigning tasks, leaders should never assume that the desired standards are already known to the followers.

When to Do It

- When your soldiers appear willing, and are trying, but their performance doesn't meet the standards required for mission accomplishment.
- When you have a new task to get done and the standards are unclear or have not yet been established.
- When soldiers ask a lot of questions or seem confused about expected outcomes.

How to Do It

- Read through some Soldier's Manuals to get a good idea of *how* standards should be stated.
- Check appropriate publications to see if standards for tasks, tech-

niques, or procedures are already clearly established—(TMs, FMs, Soldier's Manuals, SQTs, etc.).

- When standards aren't specified, *you* figure out what they should be.
- Make sure standards are *specific* and measurable whenever possible.
- Communicate standards to the soldier. *Show* him the standards if you can.
- Check to see if the soldier understands the standard.
- Hold soldiers accountable for the standards.
- Measure performance against the *stated* standards, rather than against other soldiers or teams.
- When soldiers are not able to meet desired standards right away, don't *lower* standards; establish intermediate ones. (Intermediate standards should lead step-by-step to the desired standard but be within the capability of the soldier to perform at this time.)
- When you have specified standards, *always* provide feedback to the soldier about how well he met those standards.
- Reevaluate standards when they appear to be unrealistic (too easy, too hard) after prolonged periods of training.
- If *your* leader doesn't spell out the standards when he gives you a task, then *ask* him. If *you* don't have a clear picture of what he wants, confusion will be multiplied at each level in the chain of command.

How to Know When It's Done Right

- When there are very few questions and little confusion during the course of accomplishing a task you've assigned.
- When soldiers are self-confident and proud of their work.
- When soldiers appear to be dissatisfied with poor or sloppy work.

HOW TO DELEGATE

Leaders never have enough time to do everything that is expected of them, so they have to delegate responsibility for many tasks. Simply delegating responsibility for tasks, however, does not ensure that they will be accomplished. They must be delegated to the *right* subordinates. There are some simple rules to help the leader delegate more effectively.

When to Do It

- When you find yourself falling further and further behind in your work.

- When you notice subordinates who are able and willing, but just standing around.
- When you face situations where it is impossible for you personally to supervise everyone.
- When you get the feeling you have more to do than you can handle.

How to Do It

- Divide up the overall mission into parts or tasks.
- Ask yourself, "Should this task be performed by an officer, a noncommissioned officer, or a soldier?"
- Within the appropriate category, find out who's available.
- Of those available, determine which ones have both the skill and will to perform the task.
- If you have to make a choice between skill and will, pick the soldier with the skill and check his performance frequently.
- If you don't have a soldier with the skill, show one how to do the task.
- Tell him he is *responsible* for performing the task.
- Tell him when the task must be completed, and help him with any planning or scheduling.
- Clearly describe your expectations of his performance—the standards.
- Encourage him to ask questions when he is not sure of what to do.
- Let him know that you are confident in his ability to perform the task.
- Check his performance.
- Provide necessary feedback.

How to Know When It's Done Right

- When everyone is working and busy.
- When you find that *you* have more time to supervise today's work and to plan tomorrow's work.
- When your unit completes more and more tasks in an acceptable manner.

HOW TO INSPECT

Effective leaders continually check subordinates to ensure that the *tasks* they're working on are being performed correctly—to standards and on time. Though there are many different kinds of checks that a leader can use, one of the most thorough and effective techniques is *inspecting.* Inspecting might seem like an easy task, but it's not. When a leader inspects, "doing the right things right" gets super-critical. Leadership-wise, inspections are "prime time."

Inspections can have a powerful positive effect on individuals, teams, units. They can also have a powerful negative effect. Troops work hard to get ready for inspection. Leaders "owe" it to their subordinates to be as ready to *do* the inspections as the troops are to *get* inspected.

When to Do It

- When you want to ensure *uniform compliance* with established standards and proper operating procedures (training, maintenance, supply, etc.).
- When you want to check current "as-is" status. (This is the primary purpose of making "unannounced" inspections. Unannounced inspections also save preparatory time.)
- When the situation seems to require a thorough, detailed check—when, for instance, a critical exercise or test is coming soon, or when something needs a complete, top-to-bottom checkout.

How to Do It

- Prepare for the inspection. At your level, this means *expert* knowledge on your part.
- Learn the established standards and requirements.
- Have a *plan* for inspecting. Rehearse what you're going to do. Troops will be watching you like hawks for any little screw-up.
- Inform your soldiers (well ahead of time) of the details of *what* is to be inspected, *where* the inspection will be held, *when* it will occur, *who* will inspect, and *why* the inspection is being done. Announce it, explain it, *and* post instruction on the bulletin board.
- Conduct the inspection. Keep it formal, businesslike.
- Pay attention to *detail.*
- Check what you see against established standards (you *must know* these standards).
- Record deficiencies and the responsible individuals or teams.
- Check that items are serviceable and not in need of repairs. Don't just look. Check to see that items also *work.* To do this, you have to know how to "work" the items yourself.

- Analyze the results. For example, check results against previous inspections to see whether things are getting better or worse.
- *Plan* corrective action—who, what, and by when.
- Communicate inspection results to subordinates—a detailed critique. This is the feedback to the troops and it can be a powerful leadership exercise if you do it right. Prepare as carefully as you do for a class.
- Reinspect if *you're* not satisfied with the results. If you're not satisfied with what you've seen, and you do not reinspect, then no matter what you *say,* you have automatically lowered the standards. Never hesitate to reinspect, no matter how hard you and the troops have worked.

How to Know When It's Done Right

- When individual and organizational equipment is on hand and being properly maintained.
- When you see uniformity of appearance and performance.
- When established policies and procedures are being followed and established standards are being met.
- When individuals, teams, and units can adequately perform their mission.

HOW TO MAINTAIN
GOOD PERFORMANCE LEVELS

Leaders typically pay most attention to outstanding performers and substandard ones. The soldier who simply does his job is often forgotten. However, *all* soldiers need proper supervisory recognition to maintain performance levels. What is "proper recognition"? When a leader tells an average soldier, "You're doing a good job," this often leaves the soldier wondering why the leader said it. Since the comment isn't specific, the soldier isn't able to relate it to any particular action. There are some guidelines, however, that are particularly useful when attempting to motivate the plain ol' good, average soldier.

When to Do It

- When soldiers first start meeting standards. At this stage, they need a lot of recognition.
- When soldiers have been performing at acceptable levels for some

time. (When they reach this stage, they need *periodic* recognition to let them know they're doing OK.)

How to Do It

- Always identify a *specific* aspect of a soldier's performance that is above average and tell him *why* it deserves special recognition.
- Tell your soldiers *you* appreciate their performance.
- Occasionally ask your soldiers if there is anything you can do to help them do their job better.
- Once the average soldier begins to perform well in some areas, express your confidence in his ability to perform *all* aspects of the job in the same way.

How to Know When It's Done Right

- When performance continues to meet or exceed standards.

HOW TO PROVIDE CORRECTIVE FEEDBACK TO A SOLDIER

Leaders must give their soldiers feedback in order to help them learn and to overcome substandard performances. Frequently, however, when discussing job-related problems with a subordinate, a leader may put the soldier on the defensive. Typical defensive reactions will be the following: denial, blaming someone else, reacting aggressively, offering excuses, and reacting emotionally. The soldier doesn't "own up" to his own substandard performance. The best way for a leader to avoid this is to focus his feedback on the *task*—on what the soldier *did,* not on the traits of the soldier himself.

When to Do It

- Whenever a soldier's performance fails to meet a standard.

How to Do It

- Focus as much as possible on the soldier's *performance* rather than

133

his personality or attitude. Here are examples of focusing on personality or attitude—the *wrong* approach:

"Specialist Jones, you have been extremely uncooperative lately."

"You just aren't organized."

"Smith, you are a lousy soldier."

"You have a bad attitude."

Here are examples of focusing on performance—the *right* approach:

"PVT Smith, your squad worked extra hours last week cleaning up their living area and you didn't do anything to help."

"SGT Witt, your Motor Pool maintenance procedures suffer from a lack of proper prioritizing and planning. You always wait until you get a vehicle torn apart before you check to see if you need to order a necessary part."

"SGT Lucas, until recently, you used to arrive at the supply room early enough to make sure everything was ready for issue before the troops arrived. Lately, you've been arriving after the troops, causing the whole outfit delays in the entire training schedule."

- When you evaluate a soldier's performance, always evaluate that performance against the established *standard*, not against the performance of other soldiers.

How to Know When It's Done Right

- When the soldier can tell you exactly what performance of his you have judged as poor, *and* when he can tell you *why* it is poor and what he's going to do about it.

HOW TO REWARD INDIVIDUALS

Rewards are the most powerful tool available to leaders for motivating their subordinates. Reward shows a soldier that he did a thing *right*. Punishment shows a soldier that he did a thing *wrong*. Punishment can't show him what's right; it can only show him what's wrong. Sometimes, a leader wants a soldier to *know* what's wrong, but most of the time a leader wants him to know what's *right*. What all this means is that, in terms of getting the mission accomplished, reward is more effective and takes less time than punishment. In addition to that, rewards help increase the confidence and trust between soldier and leader—confidence and trust necessary for successful battlefield performance.

When to Do It

- When a soldier has met or exceeded a *standard* for performance.

  (A SPECIAL NOTE: Some leaders will tell you they reward *only* their "best" soldiers. That's not the way to reward. It's fine to occasionally recognize your best soldiers, but make sure along the way that you are also rewarding the other soldiers who meet your standards. Your objective is to develop a unit, a whole team, where *all* soldiers meet performance standards. Everyone can be *good,* but everyone can't be *best.* Show your *good* soldiers that you value their performance, too.)

How to Do It

- Make sure that the soldier is due a reward, that his performance has met or exceeded the performance standard.

- Select a reward for the soldier based upon these factors:

  If you promised him a specific reward, give it to him. Don't make promises or hint around about rewards unless you *know* you can deliver.

  Make sure the reward means something to the soldier—that he *values* what you have promised him or given him.

  Remember that rewards take many forms—a "Good work!" a "Thank you," a pat on the back, an afternoon off, a pass, recognition in front of other soldiers, an official letter of appreciation, a good efficiency report, or a medal. Use them all.

  Fit the reward to the performance. You wouldn't give a soldier a three-day pass for passing his SQT, but you certainly ought to tell him you're proud of him.

- Follow through. Make sure that your soldiers get the rewards they deserve. Whenever possible, do the rewarding in front of other soldiers, especially members of the same team.

- Give the new guy some extra attention as far as rewarding goes. Because he *is* new, he's trying extra hard to learn what's the *right* way to do things. For him, almost any reward will have extra value.

How to Know When It's Done Right

- The soldier's performance of the tasks you assign continues to meet or exceed the standards you establish.

HOW TO BRING SMOKE

Punishment should be used as a last resort to improve the performance of soldiers. There are several reasons for this. Punishment doesn't teach a soldier what he should do. Instead, it teaches him that he should avoid getting *caught* when he doesn't do what he should do. Punishment might also lead to hate, which makes it pretty difficult to build trust, respect, and a sense of teamwork between a soldier and his leader. Finally, repeated punishment tells a man he's a "loser." This means extra work for you if you're trying to develop soldiers who have confidence that they can WIN. But don't let anyone tell you that punishment should *never* be used. It has its place, it works, and it should be used when necessary to improve the performance of your soldiers.

When to Do It

- Punish a soldier for poor performance when *all* of the following conditions have been met:

  The soldier has failed to meet a performance standard which he knew about.

  You are convinced the soldier is *unwilling*—he just doesn't appear to be trying to perform the task.

  The soldier has been warned that he will be punished if he fails to perform to the standard this time.
- Punish a soldier for violation of a specific order when you *know* that he knew about the order and you *know* he violated it.
- Punish a soldier for violation of the law ("criminal acts" such as assault, insubordinate conduct, being drunk and disorderly, etc.) when you have enough evidence to convince you that he violated the law.

How to Do It

- Make sure that the soldier should be punished, that the WHEN TO DO IT conditions have been met.
- Select a punishment for the soldier based on the following factors:

  The punishment must be *legal.* You can't violate the UCMJ or regulations, policies, and SOP when you punish a soldier.

  If you promised the soldier a specific kind of punishment, *keep your promise* and give it to him.

Select punishments that your soldiers want to avoid—not necessarily what *you* would want to avoid. Taking away a young soldier's free time by restricting him might be a much more effective punishment than taking away some of his money with a fine.

Fit the punishment to the performance. The more serious the soldier's wrong actions, the tougher the punishment should be. You should save your heavy punishments for soldiers who have committed serious acts, or for those who have continually failed to perform to standard.

- Apply punishment *as quickly as possible* after the poor performance. Make sure the soldier fully understands that the punishment is a direct result of a specific poor performance.
- Follow through. When you tell a soldier he will be punished, make sure he is.
- When the punishment has been completed, move on. Don't continually remind the soldier about it. Watch carefully to see if his performance improves.

How to Know When It's Done Right

- The soldier's behavior and duty performance improve.

HOW TO HANDLE A "SHARPSHOOTER"

One problem soldier that just about every young leader faces is the "sharpshooter"—a soldier who seems to get pleasure from making others, especially leaders, look bad. A "sharpshooter" must be handled very carefully. You can lose the respect of other soldiers if a "sharpshooter" gets the best of you. But you've got to take care of him. Make sure the soldier *is* a "sharpshooter" before you treat him like one.

When to Do It

- The soldier probably is a "sharpshooter" if:

He normally makes suggestions publicly so others can hear. (He rarely makes a suggestion to you in private.)

He seems to time his suggestions to make you "look bad." He waits until you have committed yourself to a course of action, then he suggests a "better" course of action to the group.

How to Do It

- Respond to the "sharpshooter" in a calm manner in front of others. If his suggestion is good, then go along with it, but make him do all or most of the work. If the suggestion isn't good, tell him you have decided to do things another way.

- At the first opportunity, call the "sharpshooter" aside. Tell him clearly that:

  You know what he is and why he acts the way he does. (He has a need to be the "center of attention" and to look good by making others look bad.)

  You will encourage future suggestions from him, but they should be made in a "positive" manner, either privately or at appropriate times before other soldiers.

- If the soldier "sharpshoots" again, respond to his suggestions with a response like "that might be interesting" or "we may do that some day," while at the same time, showing a lot of interest and support for the suggestions of *other* soldiers.

- AVOID A CONFRONTATION with a "sharpshooter" in front of other soldiers. If a confrontation begins to develop, remove the "sharpshooter" to a place where he can not be seen or heard by other soldiers. Deal with him as a soldier who is "unwilling" to perform in a proper manner.

How to Know When It's Done Right

- The soldier "sharpshooter" begins to make most suggestions in private or at suitable times in front of others.

HOW TO COUNSEL

A critical part of a leader's job is to counsel soldiers who have problems. Effective counseling helps the soldier understand what his own problem is, then helps him get started doing something about it. The leader's goal in counseling is to *make the soldier more effective on the job.* The objective of all counseling sessions is to help the soldier solve his own problem. Counseling is a complex skill and is an important part of a leader's duties.

When to Do It

- When the soldier's attitude or actions have changed markedly and you think he may be having problems that require your help in solving.
- When a subordinate leader brings a soldier to you for counseling.
- When a soldier himself asks you for your help or advice.

How to Do It

- Make yourself *available*. Don't just schedule "open door" time or tell your men, "Come see me if you got any problems." Get out and make yourself available.
- Don't ignore or joke about soldiers with problems. Try to build a reputation of dealing with your soldiers' problems honestly and fairly and effectively.
- Listen. Stay quiet and let the soldier do the talking.
- Take your time, be patient.
- Get the soldier to state his problem specifically. Ask him, "Can you tell me more?" Tell him, "I don't understand what you mean by so and so," or "Would you give me an example of that?"
- If you think that something can be done about the problem, then work with the soldier to reach agreement on what *he* should do to solve it. If you don't think something can be done, tell the soldier that.
- Keep on the subject.
- Make sure the conversation focuses on what the *soldier* wants to talk about. Your own war stories don't usually help *him* very much.
- Gather as much information about the soldier's problem as possible.
- Have the soldier explain points in greater detail if necessary.
- Don't get mad or argumentative about what he says. Keep on *listening*. Let *him* talk.
- At this point, think about all you've been listening to and determine whether the soldier needs some special help. You should send him for special help *only* if:

    The problem is too difficult for you.

    There is a language or cultural barrier between you and the soldier.

    You think you are not making any progress.

    You think you are too personally involved in the problem.

    He obviously needs expert knowledge that you don't have.

- If you send him to someone else, then *you* make the appointment for him.

- Check to make sure the soldier keeps his appointment.
- Talk to him after his appointment to make sure that he believes he's getting the help he needs.
- If you work with the soldier yourself, follow up on the counseling session:

  Make sure he does those things that he has told you he would do to solve his problem.

  Require him to establish intermediate goals if necessary.

  Check on his progress from time to time. Each time, get him to talk. You *listen.*

How to Know When It's Done Right

- When the soldier tells you or his leader that the problem is solved.
- When the attitude or actions that first led you to suspect that there was a problem start changing for the better.
- When the soldier returns to duty from an appropriate referral agency, *and* there is a change in his attitude and actions.

HOW TO USE THE EER AND OER TO IMPROVE PERFORMANCE

Soldiers *always* want to know where they stand. Since promotion and pay are tied to performance levels, this is a particularly critical responsibility of leaders. A leader must evaluate the performance of each subordinate continually, giving him the positive and negative feedback that is necessary to improve performance. This process of evaluation and feedback is an important part of the requirement to submit formal evaluations (EERs and OERs). There are some simple rules you can follow that will help you in conducting these performance counseling sessions.

When to Do It

- When the Army personnel system requires formal evaluations of soldier performance. To wait until a written report is due, however, is an injustice to the soldier and will probably not have the desired effect on his performance. The leader should provide feedback to the subordinate regarding his performance a *minimum* of three or four times during the rating period. Soldiers should *never* be surprised by what is written on their efficiency reports.

How to Do It

- Prepare in advance by reviewing the subordinate's job requirements.
- Get *facts* upon which to base your overall evaluation of the subordinate's performance. Continually keeping notes on the performance of subordinates is the most effective way to do this. It is also the most fair way for your soldiers.
- Give your subordinate enough time to prepare for the counseling session.
- Set aside some private, uninterrupted time for the session.
- Welcome the subordinate. Put him at ease.
- Explain the purpose of the counseling session.
- Ask the subordinate to tell you about his own performance.
- Compare this with your evaluation of his performance. If it doesn't match up, back up your evaluation with facts. Focus on *performance* more than attitude.
- Get the subordinate to identify ways to improve performance.
- Make sure the subordinate agrees to take immediate specific action.
- Keep the talk positive. Don't cut the subordinate down.
- Write up your evaluation.
- Follow through on the subordinate's progress.
- Provide necessary intermediate performance feedback.

How to Know When It's Done Right

- When subordinate performance holds steady or improves.

HOW TO CHECK UNIT PERFORMANCE

Leaders are responsible for the performance of their units. Somebody once said, "Soldiers do well what their leader checks." That's good leadership guidance. In any case, *checking* is the only way you can be *sure* that your unit *understands* your orders and your standards and is doing the right things right.

When to Do It

- Check your unit's performance constantly.

How to Do It

- Watch formal performance indicators, like SQT, ARTEP, and AGI results. More importantly, look for changes in the *overall* manner of performance of soldiers in your unit. Look for changes over *time.*
- Keep your eyes open. Move around your area both in garrison and in the field, *watching* and *listening* to what your soldiers are doing and how well they are doing it.
- Keep your ear to the ground. Listen to the "grapevine" in your unit, and make sure your other leaders do this too. As the leader, you must know *more* about what's going on in the unit than any other member.
- Go out and physically CHECK things that need to be checked. The priorities coming through your chain of command give you guidance for what to check.
- Check things that you *must* check. Regulations and SOP require you to check certain things (e.g., you must inventory weapons). *Always* make required checks. Someone else is depending on you to make a specific check. If required checks don't make sense, or there are too many, go to the chain of command.
- Check things that are *critical* to the mission. For example, if you're going to the field in cold weather, check to make sure soldiers have their cold weather clothing.
- Check subordinates who *need* to be checked. Subordinates who are unwilling and unable require constant checking; subordinates who are able and willing need to be checked very little.
- As you do your planning about "What to do next," get in the habit of *writing down* checklists in your notebook.

How to Know When It's Done Right

- There are *very* few instances when someone in your unit lets you down.
- Required material and equipment are available when you need them.
- Troops and teams don't stand around waiting and wasting time because of one or two items of equipment that didn't show up or one or two key individuals who never got the word.

HOW TO PROVIDE FEEDBACK TO TEAMS

One of the biggest problems that can occur in a team or unit is "poor communication." You've heard that before, and it's right. There are many things a leader can do to solve communication problems within his *team.* One of the best techniques is *group feedback.*

When to Do It

- A squad leader should provide feedback concerning squad performance to the members of his squad at the end of *each day* that the squad works *together.*
- A platoon leader should provide feedback concerning platoon performance to his squad leaders at the end of *each day* that the platoon works *together.* The platoon sergeant should be present.
- A unit commander should provide feedback concerning unit performance to his platoon leaders at the end of *each day* that the unit works *together.* The First Sergeant and platoon sergeants should be present.

How to Do It

- Start the session by limiting the time. Tell your subordinates that no more than ten minutes will be spent talking with the *group.* Any individual matters can be handled later on an individual basis.
- Tell your subordinates how well (and/or how poorly) you feel the day's activities went. Here's some good guidance for how to do this:

Use phrases like "It looked to me like . . ." rather than "This is what happened. . . ." Remember that you are describing what *you* saw. Someone else may have seen things differently.

Describe the performance you saw in terms of what met standards and what didn't. Emphasize timing and teamwork and mutual support. Avoid trying to describe attitudes or what people were thinking. Stay with what you *saw* or *heard.* Once you have described performance that, in your opinion, indicates a problem, then let your subordinates discuss with you what the possible causes of the problem were.

Focus on how to improve performance, *not* on trying to find out who was to blame. Blame doesn't get the mission done. Improving performance does. *Later,* find out who was to blame and correct him or punish him. Do *not* use this team session time for a group "chewing-out." Make that a "special" occasion.

Try to balance feedback with good *and* bad points. Lay out the problems you saw, but also mention performances that met or exceeded standards. Say things such as: "The overall performance was good, but I saw some things we need to talk about . . ." or, "By the way, the platoons showed real enthusiasm. The company needs that, and I want you to pass on to them that I saw it and liked their hustle."

If one of your subordinates raises a suggestion or question that cannot be fully discussed in the ten-minute period, make specific arrangements to talk to that subordinate later.

If none of the subordinates has anything to say during your discussion (the communication is one way—you to them), encourage them to comment or ask questions. If no one ever comments, you've got a problem. For some reason they don't want to talk with you. Look into a situation like this.

In cases where the entire unit performed together, like on an ARTEP, hold sessions from company level on down to squad level. But *don't* let these sessions turn into "the-CO-said-this" meetings. You want soldiers thinking and talking among themselves about *their* performance at each team level.

Listen to what your subordinates say to you. Take a few notes. In many cases, this is good feedback for you from the men who are on the receiving end of *your* leadership. *Listen,* and learn. If these sessions are handled properly, you find out a lot about what your subordinates think you do well and what they think you need to do better.

How to Know When It's Done Right

- There is little argument about who is to blame for problems. Discussion is on how to get problems *solved.*
- Your subordinates comment freely about how they evaluated performance of their team.
- You see subordinates working, on their own, to improve performances discussed during previous group feedback sessions.

HOW TO USE TEAM REWARDS

Normally, you should reward soldiers for good performance as *individuals.* However, it is important to reward *teams* (crews, squads, or platoons) from time to time, because this helps build teamwork among your soldiers.

When to Do It

- Use team rewards when members of a crew, squad, or platoon must work together to perform a task successfully or meet a team objective. In addition, such tasks or team objectives should meet the following conditions:

Each member of the team has a specific set of responsibilities which he must perform if the team as a whole is to be successful.

The performance of each soldier in the team can be seen or known by others—no member of the team is pulled out just to make the team "look" good.

The task you want the team to perform is important in terms of your unit's mission.

How to Do It

- Select a reward that meets the following conditions:

  All members of the team value the reward.

  All members of the team will share equally in the reward.
- Explain what the reward for good performance will be *before* the team begins performing.
- Clearly explain the standard that must be met before the team can receive the reward.
- Be sure that the standard is met before you give the reward.
- Follow through. Make sure each member of the team receives the reward you have promised.

How to Know When It's Done Right

- When soldiers in the team appear more enthusiastic when performing the task.
- When individual soldiers in the team apply pressure on their buddies to perform better, and when the team polices itself.

HOW TO USE TEAM PUNISHMENT

Most of the time, you should punish soldiers for poor performance as *individuals,* even when that poor performance occurred as part of a team. However, in certain cases, team punishment may be necessary to encourage better teamwork in the future. Use team punishment only when absolutely necessary, but be prepared to use it when you have to.

When to Do It

- Team punishment should be used only when *all* of the following conditions are met:

145

In the past, there has been regular and consistent punishment for poor performance—to include team punishment.

Performance of the task occurs in a team setting where members of the team can identify those who are performing poorly.

Soldiers in the team recognize that individually they can do something to avoid the punishment (working better together, prodding others to perform better, etc.).

The task is important to performing the organization's mission.

How to Do It

- Select a punishment that meets the following conditions:

  All members of the team want to avoid the punishment.

  All members of the team will share equally in the punishment if they perform poorly.

- Clearly explain the standards of performance to the team before they begin their performance. Tell them what they must do to ensure they are not punished.

- Warn the team about the punishment, and tell them exactly what the punishment will be for poor performance.

- Check performance carefully to ensure that the performance meets the standard. If it does meet the standard, reward the team. If it doesn't meet the standard, then apply the punishment you promised.

- Follow through. Make sure punishment you have applied is carried out for *all* members of the team.

How to Know When It's Done Right

- When soldiers in the team work hard to avoid the punishment.
- When individual soldiers in the team apply pressure on their buddies to perform better. The team polices itself.

HOW TO MOTIVATE

"Motivation" does not require an elaborate definition. It is simply the set of needs and wants that an individual has. These needs and wants cause him to act in a certain way. So motivation is the underlying basis for what individuals think and *do*. Individuals act in their own best interest. Maximum effort is obtained when soldiers are working toward unit goals that *also* achieve their own needs. Soldiers can be motivated internally, as well as externally, by a leader. To use motivation effectively, leaders need to recognize that: soldiers are complex and variable; they change their behavior over time (not overnight); they look for variety in their work; they want to do worthwhile things (like training); and they react differently to leadership practices. KNOWING YOUR MEN takes a lot of listening, watching, thinking. Do it well, and you can "motivate."

When to Do It

- Leaders should be attempting to motivate subordinates *continually*.

How to Do It

- Always pay close attention to the basic, physical things soldiers need —food, shelter, clothing.
- Talk with your soldiers—*listen* to them.
- Identify the things that are important to them—*their* needs.
- Evaluate how well accomplishing the mission will satisfy these needs. Explain this to subordinates.
- Set the example in everything you do, especially military skills.
- Reward *only* those who earn it.
- Punish *all* of those who deserve it.
- Promote good men and send good men to school, even when it means you might lose them.
- Explain how important their competence is to the Army and the nation, and what the people of the nation expect of their soldiers.

How to Know When It's Done Right

- A soldier's behavior changes in the desired direction.

HOW TO PREPARE FOR STRESS

Leading soldiers during battle is probably the toughest challenge anyone can face. The danger, fear, lack of sleep, and constant tension all put enormous strains on bodies and minds. Battle involves high stress. Effective performance under such high stress conditions requires preparation *before* men meet those conditions.

When to Do It

- Build activities that prepare your soldiers for stress into *all* unit activities. Training time is the *best* time for working in an element of high stress.

How to Do It

- Condition your soldiers and condition yourself. Build stress endurance through physical exercise. Soldiers preparing for combat (yours *are*, right now) should run at least thirty minutes a day or do equivalent amounts of other continuous-type exercise. For leaders, SETTING THE EXAMPLE is particularly important in this kind of endurance training.
- DRILL under conditions that are close to those you'll see on the battlefield. Make training as realistic as possible. *Practice sleeping in shifts during overnight exercises. Ensure that soldiers in your squads can work together so as to permit each one an opportunity for sleep.* Most young leaders, and some older leaders, screw up their decision making *and* their units by trying to stay awake around the clock.
- Ensure that you and your soldiers eat balanced diets—but don't overdo it. Check to see that each member of your unit gets the proper amount of food for his size and level of physical activity.
- Quickly identify and refer soldiers with alcohol and drug problems to professional help. Under battle conditions, soldiers with these problems will be among your first stress casualties.
- Familiarize your soldiers with the sounds of weapons and equipment they will hear during the battle. Give them a chance to hear U.S. artillery, mortars, and small-arms fire, and movement of U.S. vehicles. Then give them a chance to see and hear *enemy* weapons and equipment so they are familiar with the main things that cause stress on the battlefield.
- Look for every occasion to express confidence in their leaders, weapons, equipment, and training.
- Explain carefully to your soldiers that everyone has fear during battle. They must know that when they experience fear, they're experiencing the same thing as the other soldiers around them. TELL THEM THEY CAN OVERCOME FEAR BY CONCENTRATING ON THE MISSION— AND ON WHAT THEY MUST DO TO SUPPORT THEIR BUDDIES.

How to Know When It's Done Right

- The final test occurs during the battle—how well your soldiers fight, and how many fall out because they can't handle the high stress conditions of the battlefield. Before the battle, look for the following indicators:

  Your soldiers are in good physical condition.

  Your soldiers perform well during DRILL in the field.

  Under normal conditions in the field, all soldiers and subordinate leaders get an opportunity to sleep each day—and they use it.

HOW TO HANDLE FEAR ON THE BATTLEFIELD

Fear is a normal, natural human reaction to the battlefield. However, if not controlled by the leader, fear can destroy the ability of a unit to perform its mission. Fear can paralyze an individual soldier. This paralysis can then spread like wildfire, until *panic* sets in and all organized combat action ceases. This is a real threat, particularly on the modern battlefield. The use of nuclear weapons and chemical agents by the enemy increases the chances that you and your soldier will face high levels of fear. As a leader, you have to be ready to deal with fear at all times—your fear and the fear of others around you.

When to Do It

- The minute fear begins to show in the actions of your soldiers. Look for:

  A decrease in the level of activity, such as volume of suppressive fires, from your soldiers.

  Ineffective fire. Soldiers don't appear to be trying to hit enemy or fire in their primary sectors—they fire in an uncoordinated, uncontrolled manner.

  Unexplained fatigue or unresponsiveness.

- At advanced stages of fear, when previous actions to control fear have been unsuccessful. Look for:

  A soldier or small group of soldiers leaving their positions in an attempt to run to safety.

  A soldier or small group of soldiers refusing an order from a leader.

How to Do It

- Respond quickly. Fear can spread rapidly and create panic conditions in your unit. Stay alert for the ones spelled out above.
- Take visible action. SET THE EXAMPLE for your soldiers. Stay cool. Make sure that soldiers know *what* you are doing and *where* you are, all the time. Talking is one of the best methods for drawing attention to your actions. Some one or two of you who read this book will, one of these days, shoot (in the legs) some panic-stricken soldier running to the rear, and by doing so, you will save the lives of a *unit*.
- Get men "talking it up" with each other. Contact among men holds down fear and keeps teamwork going.
- Insist on combat performance. Never indicate to your soldiers that their combat performances can be "negotiated" with you. No deal. We *all* fight.
- Use special handling for "combat refusals." These individuals will be almost nonexistent in a well-prepared unit. However, a soldier who tells his leader that he "refuses" to go forward is at the first stage of being paralyzed by fear. Act quickly, and you can "cure" him. Threats of courts-martial, or talk about disgracing unit, family, nation, and so on won't work. You have to get him *started moving,* physically, *toward* the action. Four good ways to do this:

  Direct him forward to an intermediate position *partway* to the objective. That will get him started.

  Start him physically, yourself, toward the action.

  Hook him up with another soldier who is moving in the right direction; make sure this is one of your "willing and able" soldiers.

  Grab him by the arm, and take him with *you*.

- *Never* leave dead or wounded behind, even though it may cost you more casualties.
- Keep immediate treatment and evacuation of wounded high on your priority list.
- Put a skilled, trusted veteran in the *rear* of formation to keep men and small units moving forward.
- Demonstrate, by example, your own confidence. This must be done *all* the time on the battlefield. Your confidence is more important there than at any other time or place. Your confidence is the key to theirs.

How to Know When It's Done Right

- Soldiers perform quickly and effectively in response to orders.

- Suppressive fires and similar combat fire essentials are effective and maintained.
- Cases of "battle fatigue," self-inflicted wounds, lost weapons, frostbite, malaria, are at minimum levels.

HOW TO BUILD A WINNING ATTITUDE

When people talk about athletic contests, we often hear the phrase "It's not whether you win or lose, it's how you play the game." That sounds nice, but it doesn't work on the battlefield. In preparing soldiers and teams, Army leaders must operate from the position that "It's not only how you play the game, it's whether you win or lose." The contest on the battlefield is for keeps. Winning is the *only* acceptable outcome. And winning requires a winning attitude.

When to Do It

- Whenever you make decisions.
- Whenever you deal with your soldiers.

How to Do It

- When tasks are being assigned, try to convince your superiors to avoid establishing standards that, while they sound good, are beyond the capabilities of your men or the resources that are available. Setting soldiers up for certain or probable failure can give them a loser's attitude when it happens three or four times.
- SET THE EXAMPLE for your soldiers by working hard toward unit tasks and objectives. Once a mission has been assigned, demonstrate a *positive* attitude.
- Center your discussions concerning unit activities around "how to get it *done*," not "why we can't do it." NEVER stand in front of your soldiers and talk about how dumb or senseless your mission is. SET THE EXAMPLE is the most powerful leadership tool there is, but it can work just as well negatively as it can positively.
- Prepare your soldiers carefully before they set out to perform a task. Avoid requiring soldiers and teams to perform tasks for which they have not been properly trained and DRILLED.
- Make sure new soldiers are made aware of the battle history and local reputation of their unit. Pride in past achievements can make men want to win.

- Challenge other crews, squads, platoons, and companies to competition in sports or soldier skills. But don't challenge or accept a challenge until *after* you have carefully prepared your soldiers to do well.
- Reward your soldiers often. Continually tell them how important they are as individuals. Keep recognizing their good performances.
- Fight to make sure your soldiers get what they are supposed to have. Pay particular attention to obtaining a fair share of training facilities, good food, details, and time off.
- Encourage your soldiers to develop their off-duty skills—particularly sports and hobbies. Encourage skilled soldiers to compete in competition requiring use of those skills.

How to Know When It's Done Right

- Your soldiers are confident they can perform well—either in competition, against a standard, or on the battlefield.
- Your soldiers perform to standard, and they compete effectively against others. Your soldiers WIN.

HOW TO SUPERVISE

Leaders don't *do* the work. Leaders get the work done, *through the efforts of others*—and supervising is the main tool for doing this. Supervising is a complex skill. It requires leader proficiency in a whole range of specific subskills, including *all* of the leadership skills discussed in this chapter.

This "how-to" summarizes what seems to be the eight most critical skills in the one task where company-level leaders should be putting about 90 percent of their leadership effort—*supervising*.

When to Do It

- All the time.

How to Do It

- **Encourage open communications.**
  Take time to *listen* to soldiers.
  Keep soldiers informed.

Get new information out quickly.

Communicate openly and honestly.

Encourage subordinates to be open and honest.

Do not punish soldiers who tell you bad news.

- **Build teamwork.**

Provide opportunities for the group to work as a *team*.

Meet with soldiers as a group to get their ideas from time to time.

Keep the troops interested in what's going on.

Coordinate efforts of the team and show them where they depend on each other.

- **Get soldiers involved.**

Seek opinions, suggestions, and ideas of soldiers.

Be willing to make changes based on their suggestions.

Provide all subordinates an opportunity to fully use their skills on their job.

- **Encourage initiative.**

Give willing and able subordinates some freedom in how to do a job.

Use subordinates' ideas from time to time.

Use mistakes as a *learning* experience, that is, "How could you/we have done that better?"

Expect performance to be up to standards and on time without *close* checking.

Delegate to the maximum extent.

- **Provide positive supervision.**

Take care of subordinates' welfare.

Stand by subordinates for their actions.

Recognize good performance.

Get subordinates' *work* problems solved quickly and effectively.

- **Set good standards.**

Involve soldiers, when possible, in setting standards and timetables.

You set the example for "outstanding" performance.

Make standards challenging but not impossible.

Use *standards* to evaluate mission accomplishment.

- **Use control measures.**

Know what resources you have to work with, and keep track of them as the work progresses.

Establish measurable and realistic work targets and deadlines.

Adjust resources when performance measures show below-standard work.

Require soldiers to follow established SOPs, manuals, and regulations.

- **Provide performance feedback.**

  Keep subordinates informed about day-to-day work progress.

  Coach individual subordinates to improve performance.

  Evaluate individual and team performance based upon specified *standards*.

How to Know When It's Done Right

- Tasks are completed correctly and on time. The whole "climate" of your unit is such that it helps performance instead of hindering it.

HOW TO ASK THE RIGHT QUESTIONS

This last technique is the most important of the entire list we have discussed in this final chapter of how-to's. It deserves some careful explanation, and it deserves your close attention. It is a technique that applies to all the other how-to's in this book—to virtually every problem you will have to solve as a small-unit leader. Listen closely.

You get more leadership done by asking than by telling. Now, this doesn't mean you should get tasks done by asking soldiers to do them (although many times this *is* the best way). What it means is that, as a small-unit leader, the main thing you work with is people. Most of the problems you have to solve are people problems—teaching a soldier how to fire a machine gun (SKILL); motivating a soldier to want to do the right things on his own (WILL); getting soldiers and small groups of soldiers to work together (TEAMWORK).

You can't solve any of these problems without *information*. And the information you need to solve soldier problems is found in only one place —inside soldiers. To get it, you can't rely on paper—reports, records, charts, numbers. These things help—a little—but to get the information you need to solve soldier problems, you have to talk with soldiers. And when you do that, you have to know how to ask questions. Then, with the information you get by *asking,* you solve the problems and make the decisions. After all that comes the *telling.*

Few people realize it, but a leader can get many things done just with questions:

1. Get information about the soldier.
2. Get information about a subject the soldier knows.
3. Get suggestions from the soldier.

4. Find out what the soldier wants.
5. Find out his attitude toward policies and projects.
6. Get the soldier's attention.
7. Arouse the soldier's interest.
8. Get the soldier to feel at ease.
9. Make the soldier feel like a "winner."
10. Prove to the soldier that you're listening to him.
11. Show that you understand a subject important to the soldier.
12. Show the soldier you're interested in him.
13. Point out to the soldier "what's important."
14. Give yourself some time to think.
15. Help the soldier figure out his own problems.
16. Encourage the soldier to think on his own.
17. Help the soldier take responsibility for his own actions.
18. Get information about other things you're responsible for.

All those things, and a hundred more, can be done by asking—questions. Asking questions is a leader SKILL that must be studied, learned, and practiced, just like knowing how to read a map, operate a radio, or conduct training. Doing it right takes study and work. It doesn't come automatically.

Listen to a new (and maybe nervous) lieutenant asking a mortar gunner some questions during an exercise in the field. The unit's been in the position for about three hours and the mortar is still not dug in.

"Good afternoon, soldier, how's it going?"

"Just great, sir! Super field exercise!"

"Well, glad you're enjoying yourself. How long have you been occupying this position?"

"Not very long, sir."

"I see . . . well, how's your mortar; any problems?"

"No, sir . . . best mortar in the company, sir."

"Well, that's certainly good news. By the way, where are you from?"

"Texas, sir!"

"Great state to be from. It sure has provided the Army with good soldiers. Well, good talking to you, soldier. Carry on."

Now, think for a moment about what the lieutenant learned from all that. The lieutenant asked questions, and the gunner gave answers, but did the lieutenant *learn* anything? What problems can he solve with the information he got from the gunner? Next, listen to a professional, hardcore NCO talk to the same mortar gunner:

"Good afternoon, soldier. I'm Command Sergeant Major Anderson, your brigade sergeant major. And what's your name?"

"I'm PFC Little, Sergeant Major."

"Glad to meet you, Little. What outfit are you in?"

"I'm in A Company, Sergeant Major."

"I'm sure that's a fine company, Little, but which battalion?"

"3d Battalion, 8th Infantry, Sergeant Major."

"The 3d of the 8th is a fine battalion. Who's your battalion commander?"

"LTC Blanchard, Sergeant Major."

"And isn't Sergeant Major Atkins your battalion command sergeant major?"

"He sure is, Sergeant Major."

"Well, he's one of my favorite soldiers. Has been ever since we were platoon sergeants together in Vietnam. Unless he's changed, I'm sure you wouldn't want to do anything that makes him mad. I know I sure wouldn't."

"I've been lucky so far, Sergeant Major. As a matter of fact, we get along just fine."

"Well, I'm glad to hear it . . . but tell me, Little, what do you think he'd say if he saw your position like this?"

"I'd be in a world of hurt, Sergeant Major."

"Yep, I guess you would be . . . at least I wouldn't want to be in your shoes. By the way, how long have you been in position?"

"Not very long, Sergeant Major."

"OK, now tell me what 'not long' means to you . . . about how many hours ago are you talking about?"

"About three or four, I guess."

"OK, so that means you got here about 0900 this morning. Is that right?"

"Yes, Sergeant Major."

"And by the way, Little, where's the rest of your crew?"

"I can't really say for sure, Sergeant Major. I think they're maybe pulling security."

"OK, I'll check that out later. Now, what's your job in the crew?"

"I'm the gunner, Sergeant Major."

"How long have you been the gunner?"

"Almost a year."

"Well, you ought to know your job good by now. When was the last time you fired this mortar?"

"Just last month, Sergeant Major."

"Tell me more about that. How many rounds did you fire, and how long were you in the field that time?"

"We fired about twenty rounds altogether, I think, and we were in the field for three days."

"How many rounds did you fire at night?"

"Four or five."

"Any illuminating rounds?"

"No, I can't remember any."

"What were you shooting at?"

"I'm not really sure, Sergeant Major; we just took our commands from the FDC."

"OK, now tell me, Little, what additional training did you get when you weren't shooting fire missions during those three days?"

"We did SQT training, I believe."

"I see. Specifically, what kind?"

"Well, let's see . . . we talked about the Code of Conduct, and we, uh, held competition to see how fast we could disassemble and assemble our M-16s . . . and I think we also had a map reading class where we learned symbols and stuff."

"Sounds like most of that could have been taught in garrison, doesn't it? What kind of individual training did you do on the mortar itself?"

"Except for shooting it, Sergeant Major, that's about it."

"By the way, Little, what's your MOS? Are you an 11C?"

"No, Sergeant Major, actually I'm an 11 Bravo."

"How about that? Are you one of the lucky ones who was able to enlist when they were still paying 11Bs a bonus?"

"Yep. I was. As a matter of fact, I got into the Army just three days before they stopped paying the bonus."

"Well, you're fortunate. Now, tell me a little about your mortar. When you went to the field last month, did you shoot this same mortar, or another one?"

"This one, Sergeant Major."

"And how did it shoot?"

"Not all that good, Sergeant Major, too much wobble."

"What have you done to correct that problem?"

"Sent it in to maintenance . . . we just got it back last Friday."

"So it was in maintenance about a month. How many other times has it been in maintenance during the year you've been the gunner?"

"I've lost count, Sergeant Major. Seems like about half the time, at least. If it's not one thing, it's another."

"What's usually the problem?"

"Most of the time it's the sight, but sometimes it's the bipod."

"I see. OK, let me change the subject. How about explaining to me the first thing you do when you initially occupy a new position?"

"Well, let's see . . . I guess the first thing I'd do is set up local security."

"Good; and then what?"

"Dig in."

"Would you dig in before, or after, you set up your mortar?"

"Afterwards, Sergeant Major; I'd want to be ready for a fire mission as soon as possible in case our guys needed fire, so I'd set up the mortar as soon as we got some security out, then start digging and camouflaging."

"Hey, good answers, Little! Shows you're thinking. One last thing: I don't know if I'll be able to get back this way anytime soon, but if I did, how long from now do you think it might take for me to see this position completely squared away?"

"Sergeant Major, a give me another fifteen minutes and you won't even be able to see me when you come back!"

"Great! I sure enjoyed talking with you, Little. Good luck . . . and be sure to let your squad leader and platoon sergeant know I stopped by. See you later."

The Command Sergeant Major was a professional NCO. Asking questions was a skill he had developed to the point where it was instinctive and "natural." He didn't ask questions just to be asking questions. He knew what he was looking for. He wanted information on individual training, maintenance of weapons, and personnel assignments. He spent maybe twenty minutes with Little. After he's talked with five or six more soldiers like Little, he'll put what they say together with other information he's learned, and then he's ready to go start asking some more questions—this time, over in the NCO support channel. . . .

Unfortunately, the majority of leaders, from corporals to generals, don't spend the time and effort required to learn the skill of asking questions. Some ask a few questions just because they think leaders are "supposed to." Others avoid asking questions because they don't know the technical details of the answers and don't want to be embarrassed (but if you'll think back to the Command Sergeant Major's questions, you'll see that no one "graded" him on technical details!). Too many leaders feel awkward about asking questions. They may try asking a few, just for the sake of asking questions, but this invariably gives soldiers the feeling that they're trying to get the conversation over with as quickly as possible. They somehow fail to realize that asking the right questions at the right time in the right sequence is *the* best way for a leader to find out what's going on inside his soldiers.

A half-dozen good guidelines will get you started on developing the critical leader SKILL of asking questions:

1. Don't ask a soldier any questions that can be answered just with a simple "yes" or "no." Instead, ask *leading* questions that require some explanation—then listen hard between the lines as the soldier explains.
2. Don't ask a soldier any questions that might require him to be outwardly critical of his unit or chain of command. The vast majority of soldiers don't willingly want to get their leaders in trouble, even though they feel it would be justified. In other words, don't put the soldier on the spot.

3. Steer clear of vague, general questions that invariably will get you vague, general answers. Such questions serve to make conversation, but not *communication.*

4. Learn how to tactfully, indirectly, quietly, nicely challenge the "automatic positive" answers soldiers will give if they get a chance: "How's the chow, soldier?" "Just great, Sergeant (Sir)!"

5. Keep working constantly to get the soldier to elaborate, explain, amplify his answers. Get into the habit of probing: "*Why* do you think this is so?" "*When* did you last do such and such?" "*Where* did you learn that?" "*Who* taught it to you?" "*How* would you do this or that?" "*What* do you think of this policy or that requirement?" As a general rule, every other question should start with a why, when, where, who, how, or what.

6. Before asking the "hard" questions that the soldier might be hesitant to answer, set him at ease so he can feel free to explain. Don't try to pressure him or trick him or trap him. You're a leader, *not* a lawyer.

To begin developing "natural" question-asking skill, spend some time studying and *using* the **GOOD** questions listed below. They are probing or leading questions, related to the routine everyday life of the soldier, and designed to stimulate discussion so that you can get the information you need to solve leadership problems.

In each case, there's the general, vague question that many leaders would ask, followed by the usual kind of general, vague answers they would get and often be satisfied with. The "GOOD" questions are the kind the Command Sergeant Major would keep asking—to find out about the who, what, when, where, why, and how.

QUESTION	**GOOD** QUESTION
1. "How's your radio (weapon/ vehicle)?" Usual answer: "Great shape."	"When was your radio (weapon/ vehicle) in maintenance the last time? What was wrong with it? How long was it in the maintenance shop?"
2. "What's your job?" Usual answer: "I'm a mechanic (rifleman/cook, etc.)."	"What's your primary MOS? What was your score on the last SQT? How long have you been working in your present job? Are you a Bonus Recipient?"

3. "Are you going to reenlist?"
   Usual answer: "I probably will."

"When are you going to reenlist?" (or) "What convinced you to reenlist? If you aren't going to, why not? What do you think might change your mind?"

4. "What's the situation?" (To soldier in assembly area)
   Usual answer: "We are on a FTX."

"How long have you been in this assembly area? What have you been doing since you got here? What are you going to be doing next? What's the purpose for this training? What have you learned so far? When does the FTX end? Have you seen any aggressors? What were they doing? Where is your platoon CP? Your company CP? What's the password?"

5. "How are you shooting?" (To soldier on Rifle Range)
   Usual answer: "Just fine, Sir (Sergeant)."

"What's your zero? How do you know? When did you last re-zero this weapon? Did you get any preliminary rifle instruction before you came to the range? Where? When? What did you do? What was your score? Who coached you while you were firing for practice? What did that coach teach you? When was the last time you fired at night for qualification?"

6. "How's the food in your Mess Hall?"
   Usual answer: "Just fine, Sir (Sergeant)."

"How many meals do you usually eat in your Mess Hall during the week? How many on Saturday? What about Sunday? What are the Saturday Mess Hall hours? Sunday's? What did you have for supper last night? Were you able to get seconds? What did you have for breakfast? Was the bacon hot? Greasy? Did you get eggs to order? How many choices? Does the ice machine work? When was the last time it didn't? When was the last time you saw your Company Commander (First Sergeant) eat Saturday supper (Sunday dinner) in the Mess Hall?"

7. "Do you have a good squad?" (To a Squad Leader)
Usual answer: "Yes, Sir (Sergeant), you bet."

"How long have you been the squad leader of this squad? What's your MOS? How many men are assigned to your squad? How many were present for duty yesterday? How many today? How many men are SD? Where are they working? How long have they been on SD? What are the names of your married men? What are their wives' names? Where do they live? How many of your men live in the barracks? Who lives off post? How many qualified with their individual weapon? When did they qualify? What were their scores? Have any of your men had an Article 15? How long ago? For what? What was his punishment? Have any of your men ever had a pay complaint? What was the problem? What did you do about it? How long did it take? Tell me each man's score on the last PT test. What is each man's TA50 status? Tell me what each is missing. How long has he been missing those items? What have you done about it? When was the last time a man in your squad was promoted?"

8. "You being taken care of okay?" (To a soldier during inspection in ranks)
Usual answer: "Oh, yes, Sir (Sergeant), everything is fine."

"How long have you been in this company? Who is your company commander? How long has he been in command? Do you have a school degree; if not, have you had a chance to get your GED?

When were you last promoted? How long did it take you to get a copy of your promotion orders? How long did you have to wait until you started to get paid for your promotion? When did you get leave last time? How many days did you take? Can you find toilet paper in the latrine on Sunday afternoon? Do the washer and dryer in your barracks work? How often do they break down? Does the heat work in the barracks? Have you ever had anything stolen in the barracks? What? When? Did you ever get it back? How do you get paid? Have you been offered an opportunity to make out a will? Does the TV work in the dayroom? How do you find out what training is scheduled? When do you find this out? Do you get compensatory time for night or weekend training? How often do you pull guard? How about your buddies?"

9. "Do you believe your chain of command knows what's going on?"

Usual answer: "Yes."

"How much notice do you usually get before going to the field? How often do you get changes?"

10. "Does your boss tell you when you've done a good job?"

Usual answer: "Yes."

"When was the last time your squad leader (platoon sergeant/platoon leader/first sergeant/company commander) told you personally that you had done a good job? What did you do to deserve the 'Atta-boy'?"

11. "Do you like your job?"

Usual answer: "Yes," or, "It's okay."

"What do you like most about your job? What do you like least? If you could change jobs, would you? What job would you choose?"

12. "Do you understand what's expected of you in your job?" Usual answer: "Yes."

"Please tell me what your job is and how you go about doing it."

13. "Can you count on your chain of command to help you with a problem?" Usual answer: "Yes."

"When was the last time you had to ask your squad leader (platoon sergeant/platoon leader/ first sergeant/company commander) to help you with a problem? What was the problem? What did they do about it? What did you do about it?"

14. "Do your NCOs talk to you?" Usual answer: "Yes."

"When was the last time your squad leader (platoon sergeant/ first sergeant) talked to you eyeball-to-eyeball? What was the subject? Who started the conversation, you or him? How often do you get into just a one-on-one BS session with your squad leader (platoon sergeant/first sergeant/ CSM)?"

15. "Do your officers talk to you?" Usual answer: "Yes."

"When was the last time you had a one-on-one conversation with your platoon leader (company commander/battalion commander)? Who started the conversation? What did you talk about?"

16. "Do you think you are getting good training?" Usual answer: "Yes."

"What's the most exciting training you've ever had? When did you do that? What's the worst training you've ever had? Why was it the best (worst)? What training did you do last week? Why did you do that? What did you learn? What are you doing this week? Why do you need to do that? Tell me about next week."

Try three or four of these GOOD questions each day. Write 'em down in your notebook, and even peep at 'em from time to time if you have to. Keep on working through the list for about a month, and then you'll start to notice at least four *guaranteed* results: (1) you won't feel awkward about asking questions of your soldiers; (2) you'll realize that you "know your men" about ten times better than you did before; (3) you'll notice that more and more of your soldiers are trying to do things right; and (4) you'll see that, as their leader, you're doing the *right* things.

And at this point—Sergeant, Lieutenant, Captain—we have reached the end of the final chapter on the how-to's of small-unit leadership. It's time now to sit back and think about some of the things we've discussed: the purpose of leadership; Stan Goff and Bob Sanders; "able and willing"; skill and will; teamwork; Howard's Hill; and, scattered from one end of this book to the other, a hundred how-to's for solving the problems of small-unit leadership. Your job, starting now, is to talk about, ask about, read about, and PRACTICE these ideas and techniques over and over until they become natural instincts. They are the "right things" for you to do as a small-unit leader. They are RIGHT because they were selected specifically to help you do the only two things a small-unit leader is supposed to do:

- LEAD SOLDIERS AND SMALL UNITS DURING BATTLE
- PREPARE SOLDIERS AND SMALL UNITS TO FIGHT THE BATTLE

Index

Able and willing gauge, 70
Abrams, General, 19
Adams, J., 110
Anderson, Command Sergeant Major, 155–58
Answers, "automatic positive," 159
Arithmetic of leadership, 62–63
Army Noncommissioned Officer Guide, 52
Attitude, how to build a winning attitude in your unit, 151

Bad news, how to move it upward, 36
Balancing mission and men, 79–80
Battle, description, 4–5; how "battle doctrine" works, 25; Howard's Hill, 97; individual in, 13–19; small unit in, 97–110; unit battle history's importance to a "winning attitude," 151; what captains do in, 26; what colonels do in, 26; what generals do in, 25. *See also* Combat, Battlefield
Battlefield, characteristics of future, 23; conditions of, 4; indicators of fear in the small unit on, 149; soldier "values" on, 83–85; three things

that must happen in order to win on, 24–25. *See also* Combat, Battle
Bearing, three ways to set examples of, 37
Best, not always good, 58; not equal to "most," 23
Binns, R., 100
Blair, J., 104
Brown, J., 109
Buddy, 83
Butler, S., 105

Candor, as a battlefield value, 83
Carlis, I., 110
Castile, Hardcore, 20
Chain of command, as primary mechanism for information flow, 48–52; communication not "violation," 36; how it works, 47; importance of working through, 48; on the battlefield, 47; what it does, 3, 47
Checking unit performance, 141
Cliques, 75
Cohesive unit, how a soldier feels in one, 10
Combat, "cohesion" as the soldier

165

Moser, R. É., 105
Motivation, because of the NCO's
interest and competence, 13; how to
build high morale and esprit, 80; of
subordinates, 146; of soldier in combat, 3; importance of listening, 147;
rewards as, 134. *See also* Will

NCO, conducting individual training in
the field, in combat, 12; development
plan, 78; duties and responsibilities,
52–53; examples of professional,
hardcore, 155–58; relationship
between officer and NCO duties,
52–53; the *Army Noncommissioned
Officer Guide,* 52; support channel,
52
Needham, Sergeant, 20
Notebook, small-unit leader's, 121,
126, 141

Officer-NCO relationship, 53
Open-door policy, 36
Orderly room, typical day, 54–56
Orders, giving, 46; how to check to
see if understood, 51
Organizational Leadership, based on
teamwork among the levels of leadership in the unit, 28; explained,
27–28; how differs from individual
leadership, 27–28; provides an
"extra" to the unit, 27
Orientation, of "the new guy," 74–76

Paperwork, when to do it, 126
Parfox (parapet foxhole), 89
Performance, basic "formula" for individual, 62; basic "formula" for unit,
62; how to check unit, 141; how to
get a soldier to "own up" to substandard, 133; how to maintain good
levels, 132
Perryman, J. M., 102
Planning, guide for, 45
Principles of Leadership, as mixture of
research and experience, 32; guidelines for application, 32–34; listed,
32–34
Priorities, five ways to develop a

"sense of priority," 59–61; how to
calibrate with leader's, 59–60; how
to handle changing, 59–60; role of
NCO support channel in keeping
aligned, 59–60; sense of, 58; using
established standards to allocate
effort, 58
Processing information, how to, 121
Punishment, how to give it to individuals, 136; how to give it to teams,
145

Questions, eighteen things a leader
can get done with, 154; four guaranteed results of asking the right,
164; how to ask the right, 154; leading, 158; probing, 159; six guidelines for asking the right, 158–59

Radio-telephone procedure, why
important, 48
Recognition, how to give, 132
Redic, T., 107
Reed, D., 99
Relief of a leader, 79
Replacement, how to bring new sol-
dier into the unit, 74–76
Reward, how to give to individuals,
134; how to give to teams, 144
Roth, S., 109

Sanders, Bob, 5, 21
Satisfaction, what makes soldiers
"satisfied" with being soldiers,
68–69
Selflessness, three ways to set
examples of, 39
Self-starter, how to be one, 123
Sense of priority, how to develop, 58
Sergeant's business, described by
sergeant, 35; in terms of officer-
NCO relationship, 53; example of
how it works in the unit, 57–58
Service, meaning of, 3
Sharpshooter, how to handle, 137
Shields, J. M., 102
Skill, how to size up individual soldier's
skill and will, 70–71; leader's "inven-

Col. Dandridge M. (Mike) Malone, U.S. Army (Ret.)

Malone began his Army career as a private and ended as a colonel almost thirty years later. During that time, he gained a B.S. degree from Vanderbilt University and an M.S. from Purdue, and graduated from the Army's Command and General Staff College and the Army War College. Renowned as the Army's leading expert on leadership, both in garrison and in combat, he has taught the subject to noncommissioned officers, West Point cadets, and students at various Army service schools to include the Army War College. An audiotape he prepared on leadership, *Soldier,* has some fifty thousand copies in circulation among Army troop units worldwide, and has brought Malone's lessons on leadership to every battalion and brigade commander assigned to command within the past four years. Retired in 1981, he resides in Florida where he continues a healthy interest in both leadership and his well-loved Army.